Contents

CONTENTS

CONTENTS

CONTENTS

Special thanks to the following
for providing the spectacular color
photography that made this book possible:

Coins

Heritage Numismatic Auctions, Inc.
3500 Maple Ave., 17th Floor
Dallas, TX 75219-3941
214-528-3500
800-US COINS (872-6467)
Bid@HeritageCoins.com
View full color images at Heritage Coins.com

Paper Money

Chester L. Krause

General Introduction

This book is not intended to be a comprehensive resource about coins and paper money. In fact, a full library is necessary to answer every question regarding this subject. Rather, it is intended to fill a much needed niche —a very basic introduction, in which a reader can get a quick overview of the hobby and get a general feel for the background, characteristics and values of each of the common categories presented.

Because this book is only an introduction to the subject, only brief information is given on early coins and paper money, and photos and listings focus on items from the early 1800s and later, which are the items most likely to be encountered today.

1884CC Gold Twenty Dollar Piece

VALUES

Coin and currency prices can be as volatile as the stock market. While some coins and bills remain stable for years, others skyrocket during a period of popularity and then plummet when they fall out of fashion. The listings presented here simply give an idea of the normal retail value at the time of writing. Because the law of supply and demand ultimately rules, the final decision about the value of a coin lies with the buyer and seller.

Dealers are in business to make a living. This means they must pay less than the retail cost listed in this book when they are buying. Depending on the value and demand, a dealer will pay between 10 percent and 90 percent of the retail value of coins or currency listed in this reference.

Finally, the grades chosen to represent average prices are those most likely found in the market or the ones most likely to be sought by the average collector.

SIZES

Coins and paper money are not shown to scale in this book. Most coins have been enlarged to show more detail, and all paper money has been reduced to fit the pages. Thus, do not rely on the size of the photos for identification, but rather the information stamped or printed on the coins or bills, and the captions and listings accompanying them.

Coin Introduction

EVOLUTION OF U.S. COINS

An average American living in the 13 colonies during the 18th century would not have found many English silver or gold coins in his pocket. It was British policy to restrict the export of precious metals to the colonies. As a result, nothing but copper was struck for the colonies, and even that was rarely minted.

Silver coins were so scarce in the Colonies that Colonial Americans used any other foreign silver or gold coin that could be pressed into service. Besides Spanish coins, French, Portuguese, and occasionally German silver and gold were readily accepted when they turned up.

French Colonies 1762A Sou Marque

1787 Continental Congress Fugio Cent

Some of the colonial governors also issued paper money valued in terms of discounted British currency, or in Spanish milled dollars. After the Declaration of Independence, many of the same forms of currency continued. Spanish colonial silver and gold were as popular as ever. All the new states issued their own paper money.

Because under the Articles of Confederation (the first United States Constitution) each state was essentially a fully sovereign country, some of them issued official state-sanctioned coinage.

When the Constitution took effect in 1789, it put an end to all state-issued coinage. In view of the new, stronger federal union, many people began to take the idea of a single national coinage more seriously. Others argued that it was not the place of government to get involved in such things. With the personal influence of George Washington himself behind them, the proponents of the new United States mint persevered, and construction began in 1792.

For both administrative and technical reasons, the mint got off to a slow start, but before the end of the year, silver five-cent pieces struck from the first president's tableware were circulating around Philadelphia. The new coinage was based on a decimal system dividing a dollar into 100 cents. The idea of the dollar as the standard unit was inspired by the Spanish piece of eight, then common in the Colonies.

Suffering under a severe shortage of both bullion and labor, as well as annual epidemics of yellow fever, the early mint never succeeded in placing substantial coinage in circulation on a national level. Broad circulation was also prevented by the rapid withdrawal and melting of much of the gold and silver coinage by speculators, because American coins had too high a precious metal content relative to their value. The endeavor became so futile that the striking of many denominations was frequently suspended. It wasn't until the 1830s that the weights of the coins were adjusted to prevent their export.

During the mint's first four decades, every die was engraved by hand, so no two looked alike. Also, the coins were struck by hand on a screw press one at a time. Finally, in 1836, the Industrial Revolution came to the U.S. Mint. Steam-powered striking equipment was imported from England. Almost overnight American coins became more neat and uniform. The old lettered edges were replaced by modern reeding, the hundreds of parallel lines found on coins today.

Also the quantities that could be produced in the same amount of time increased drastically. This technological improvement roughly coincided with the needed reduction in the coins' bullion content and with a facelift for all silver denominations. Thus, during the mid-1830s, the nation's coinage was utterly transformed.

The silver three-cent piece and three new gold denominations, $3 (1854) and $1 and $20 (1849) were introduced, partially because of the California gold rush.

1873 Silver Three-Cent Piece

1860S Gold Three Dollar Piece

But the big event of the mid-century was the coinage law of 1857. This one act eliminated the half-cent, reduced the size of the one-cent piece from bigger than a quarter to the diameter used today and, most importantly, caused foreign silver and gold to cease to be legal tender in the United States. The mint was finally able to produce enough to provide a true national coinage.

Civil War coin shortages not only resulted in many private tokens, but also inspired the two-cent and nickel three-cent pieces, and later possibly the five-cent nickel. It also saw the debut of the motto "In God we trust" on the coinage. During the late 1860s and 1870s the nation was in the economic doldrums. Mintages were low for many denominations, particularly the silver dollar, and hence many coins are scarce today.

1885 Nickel Three-Cent Piece

From the late 1870s onward, coinage was plentiful for half a century—sometimes too plentiful. A dominant political influence was the "Free Silver Movement," which didn't mean people wanted to be given free silver, but that they wanted unlimited quantities to be converted into coin to use up the excess that was being mined. They also intended that this increase the money supply, thereby causing inflation to erode debts.

From 1873 to 1918 and later, several laws were passed to force the government to buy silver and strike an abundance of silver dollars. Unpopular in the more developed parts of the country, the dollar coins frequently sat in government or bank vaults for decades. Minor silver also became more common during this era.

1879O Morgan Dollar

Early in the 20th century, Theodore Roosevelt led the nation to a new level of intellectual consciousness, touching on ideas as diverse as national parks and the artistic merits of the nation's coinage. For the latter, he sought the aid of the greatest sculptors of the day, deliberately looking outside the mint staff for talent. Most of the new coin designs reflect neo-classical artistic trends also prevalent in Europe. The beautiful designs include the Mercury dime, the Walking Liberty half, and the St. Gaudens double eagle, as well as the less classically inspired Buffalo nickel.

A commemorative coin program was also getting underway, providing an outlet for artists of various tastes. Most never saw circulation, being sold at a premium to collectors. By 1936, this had gotten so far out of hand that in that one year alone, 22 different half dollars were struck!

1942 Walking Liberty Half Dollar

1943S Zinc-Coated Steel Lincoln Cent

1943P Jefferson Nickel

The need for strategic metals for armaments during World War II was the cause for interesting, if not pleasant, aberrations in the cent and nickel. The striking of these in steel and a silver-manganese alloy respectively was a response to these shortages.

Idealistic images of Liberty were gradually replaced during the 1930s and 1940s with those of statesmen, and artists were determined by contests rather than by selection.

An increase in the price of silver in 1964 prompted massive hoarding of silver coins as their content approached their face value. As a result, silver was partially or completely removed from coinage in favor of clad coinage, which can be readily distinguished by the copper core visible on the edge. Almost 30 years later, the cent, too, was debased, the bronze alloy being replaced by one of zinc simply plated with bronze.

Today, the nation's coinage is characterized by a new flood of commemoratives struck for both significant and insignificant reasons, most completely unknown to the American people. Traditionally sold at a high premium by the mint, commemoratives circulated at face value in 1999 for the first time since the Bicentennial.

2005 Oregon State Quarter

The five 1999 state quarters were the first issues in a 10-year series commemorating each state. The state quarter series has been well received by the public and has been credited with creating significant growth in the popularity of coin collecting in the U.S.

COIN MINTS AND MINT MARKS

The first U.S. mint was constructed in Philadelphia in 1792. Over the centuries, the continuously growing facility has had several different homes in that city. Officially, all other mints are branch mints, but this does not mean that the largest quantities of each coin are always struck in Philadelphia.

The first branch mints were opened to strike coins from new gold being mined from deposits found in the South. These mints at Charlotte, North Carolina, and Dahlonega, Georgia, were opened in 1838 and closed with the Civil War in 1861. They never struck in any metal but gold, usually in small quantities. Also opened for the same duration, but of far greater importance, was the New Orleans mint. This became the second largest, striking vast numbers of coins in both gold and silver.

The San Francisco mint was opened in 1854 in response to the California Gold Rush. Today, it strikes most of the proof issues. In 1870, the silver mining boom in Nevada caused the mint to open a branch in Carson City. It was closed in 1893, and its coins are generally scarce.

Easily rivaling Philadelphia in its present importance is the Denver mint. Opened in 1906, it sometimes strikes more coins than the primary mint itself.

Recently some coins have been struck at West Point, N.Y. These are not circulation strikes, but collector issues and bullion only.

One can usually tell where a coin is struck by its mint mark, a small letter or a mark placed on the coin. In the United States, they have usually been on the reverse, but reappeared on the obverse after they were removed from 1965 to 1967. The following are mint marks used on United States coins:

none	Philadelphia
P	Philadelphia
C	Charlotte, NC
CC	Carson City, NV
D	Dahlonega, GA
D	Denver, CO
O	New Orleans, LA
S	San Francisco, CA
W	West Point, NY

COIN GRADING

The value of a coin is in part determined by its "grade," or state of preservation. The most basic part of grading is determining how much a coin is worn. To describe a coin that is not present, such as in correspondence, numismatists have agreed on a series of terms to describe how much wear there is on a coin. Following are the grades from best (no wear at all) to worst (worn out):

Uncirculated (Mint State)

Almost Uncirculated

Extremely Fine (Extra Fine)

Very Fine

Fine

Very Good

Good

Fair

Poor

For every type of U.S. and Canadian coin, very specific criteria have been agreed on for each degree of wear. For U.S. coins, these criteria were developed under the auspices of the American Numismatic Association and have been published in *Official A.N.A. Grading Standards for United States Coins*, usually called *The Gray Book*. It is carried and used by virtually every coin shop. Below are some illustrations of examples of coins in each state of wear, with some of the basic requirements for that grade.

Uncirculated (Unc.) or Mint State (MS) coins, those with no wear at all, as though they had just come from the mint, have been divided into 11 basic categories, from 60 to 70, the latter being best. The reason for this is that even with no circulation at all, the coins themselves do hit each other while stored at the mint in large bags, leaving minute scuffs. These scuffs are called "bag marks." While these 11 points are a continuum, the ANA has not traditionally recognized intermediate grades other than the ones listed below. Many coin dealers do. When a legendary numismatic scholar and cataloger was asked if he could tell an MS-61 from an MS-62, he replied "No. Neither, I think, can anyone else. It is simply ammunition for those whose motivation is dishonesty and greed."

Uncirculated or Mint State coins with absolutely no bag marks or any other problems are called MS-70, but these perfect coins do not really exist for most series. To be MS-70, a coin must be fully struck and have no unpleasant stains or discoloration.

BU (Brilliant Uncirculated) refers to a mint state coin retaining all or most of its original luster. It may have a numeric grade of MS-60 to MS-70. In the case of higher grades, many dealers prefer to use the more precise numeric grades.

MS67

MS-67 is the nearest thing to a perfect coin that is likely to be practically obtainable. It may have the faintest of bagmarks discernible only through a magnifying glass. Copper must have luster.

MS65

MS-65 is a grade describing an exceptional coin. It is the highest grade that can be easily obtained when conservative grading is used. It will have no significant bag marks, particularly in open areas such as the field or the cheek. Copper may have toning. Fewer than one coin in hundreds qualifies for this grade, and is one of the most popular grade of coins with investors.

MS63

MS-63 coins are pleasant, collectible examples that exhibit enough bag marks to be noticed, but not so many as to be considered marred, with particularly few on open areas such as the fields or a cheek.

MS60

MS-60 describes those coins that were very much scuffed up at the mint before their release. They will often have nicks and discoloration. Sometimes called "commercial uncirculated," they may actually be less pleasant to behold than a higher grade circulated coin.

AU

About Uncirculated (AU) describes coins with such slight signs of wear that some people may in fact need a mild magnifying glass to see them. A trace of luster should be visible. One should be careful not to confuse an attractive AU coin for Uncirculated.

EF

Extremely Fine (EF, XF) is the highest grade of coin that exhibits wear significant enough to be seen easily by the unaided eye. It is a coin that still exhibits extremely clear minute detail. In the case of American coins featuring the word LIBERTY on a headband or shield, all letters must be sharp and clear. Many coins will exhibit luster, but it is not necessary.

VF

Very Fine (VF) coins show obvious signs of wear. Nevertheless, most of the detail of the design is still clear. It is an overall pleasant coin. On American coins with LIBERTY on a headband or shield, all letters must be clear.

Fine (F) is the lowest grade most people would consider collectible. About half the design details show for most types. On U.S. coins with LIBERTY described above, all letters must be visible if not sharp.

VG

Very Good (VG) coins exhibit heavy wear. All outlines are clear, as is generally the rim. Some internal detail also shows, but most is worn off. At least three letters of LIBERTY described above must be legible, all letters on pre-1857 copper and Morgan dollars.

Good (G) coins are generally considered uncollectible except for novelty purposes. The design usually shows no internal detail at all. Some of the rim may also be worn out. As described above, LIBERTY is worn off on most coins and shows just trace elements on pre-1857 copper and Morgan dollars.

About Good (AG) and Fair (FR) are grades in which only truly scarce coins are collected. Many collectors would rather do without a coin than to add it to their collections. The rim will be worn down and some outline to the design may be gone.

Poor (PR) is the lowest possible grade. Many coins in Poor will not even be identifiable. When identifiable, many will still be condemned to the melting pot. Few collectors would consider owning such a coin except in the case of the most extreme rarities.

Sometimes treated as a grade, but technically not one at all is **Proof (PF)**. Proof quality is a special way of making coins for presentation. A proof coin is usually double struck with highly polished dies on polished blanks, yielding a mirror-like finish. These days, the mint mass-markets proof coins to collectors.

Proof

In the past, matte or sandblast proofs were popular, characterized by a non-reflective but highly detailed surface. Cameo proof is a particular kind of proof that has been struck with dies polished only in the fields, but with the details such as the portrait deliberately given a dull finish. For some coins, these cameo proofs have a premium value above regular proofs. Proofs often grade MS-65 or higher.

Other miscellaneous factors can affect the quality of a coin. The presence of all or part of the original luster usually increases a coin's value. Be careful, however, not to be fooled by a coin that has been dipped in a brightener to simulate this luster artificially.

Poor Toning

Toning can be good or bad. If the toning a coin has acquired is dull, irregular, or splotchy, it is likely to be considered unpleasant, and many collectors may choose to avoid it even if it is a high-grade coin.

On the other hand, if the toning is mild or displays a "halo effect" around the edge of the coin, or is composed of pleasant iridescent shades,

Ideal Toning

many collectors and dealers would consider paying a premium to obtain it based on its "eye appeal." Standard phrases used to emphasize a coin's eye appeal when grading include Premium Quality (PQ) and Proof Like (PL).

Also, the mint will sometimes strike a coin on a blank that is properly prepared enough not to be considered an error, but is nevertheless in some minor way imperfect. The poor mixing of the metals in the alloy, or flaws left by trapped gas from this same process, are examples. If trivial, they may be ignored on most coins, but on more expensive or high-grade pieces, the level of concern over these flaws may increase.

Even on circulated coins, few collectors wish to have scratches or edge nicks. These will occur even more frequently on larger coins like silver dollars or on coins with reeded edges. Depending on extent, such coins may be discounted by a little or a lot.

Of course, coins with damage are worth far less than coins without. Many coins have been mounted for use in jewelry, and even when the loop or bezel has been removed, they may still show slight signs of this unfortunate experience. A few collectors consider these situations opportunities to acquire coins with high-grade detail for a fraction of the cost. It should be remembered that the same heavy discount will apply when the collector resells the coins.

HANDLING AND TREATMENT OF COINS

How a collector or dealer treats his coins can greatly affect how well they hold their value. Metal is both more reactive and softer than most people think.

The human body contains many corrosive chemicals. In some cases, simply touching a coin can contribute to its deterioration. This is especially true of coins exhibiting mint luster or iridescent toning. Touching a bright copper surface with a sweaty thumb can easily result in the appearance of a dark thumbprint several weeks or months later.

All this being said, it is easy to understand why the first lesson of coin collecting is to ***never touch a coin on its surface.*** If one needs to pick up a coin with bare skin, touch only its edge. In the case of proof coins, even greater precaution must be taken. The highly reflective surfaces are so sensitive that one should avoid even breathing directly on a coin. This will create small black dots that coin collectors call "carbon spots." Also, do not leave coins where they can be directly exposed to dust, sunlight, or changes in temperature.

TO CLEAN OR NOT TO CLEAN COINS?

Many new collectors ask the question "How do I remove the toning?" While it can be done, it is not recommended. While there are rare exceptions when it is beneficial, it should generally be stated that one should ***never clean a coin***. It is highly likely that more harm than good will result. Toning is actually part of the coin. It is molecularly bonded to the metal, and the only way to remove the toning is to remove part of the coin. This is the way in which most coin dips work, by means of a mild acid. Physical cleaning is even worse, as microscopic striations almost inevitably are scraped into the coin's surface even using materials as mild as a tissue!

COIN STORAGE

Coins can be stored in many ways. One of the most convenient is in two-inch square plastic "flips." These are transparent holders with two pockets, one to contain the coin, one to contain a cardboard ticket on which information can be recorded. It folds over on itself into a size two inches by two inches. Originally, they were made only of a PVC formula plastic. This material was particularly flexible and easy to work with, but eventually it would break down, depositing a green slime on the coins it contained.

Today both the PVC formula and a new, more inert Mylar formula are available. The Mylar type is prone to cracking, but so far has not been found to damage coins. The PVC type is still popular because it is more flexible, but it is now usually used only by dealers and auction houses for temporary storage. Collectors usually repackage coins purchased in such holders before placing a coin into long-term storage.

Another common coin holder is the "two-by-two." This is a pair of cardboard squares with an adhering film of relatively inert plastic on one side. The coin is sandwiched between the two layers of plastic, and the two halves are stapled together. While this does not permit the coin to be removed and touched as easily as storage in flips, it does permit the coin to be viewed on both sides without opening the holder.

It is important to be very careful when removing coins from these holders so the coin is not accidentally scratched on the exposed ends of the staples that poke out when the holder is pulled apart. These careless staple scratches have ruined tens of thousands of good coins.

Both flips and two-by-twos fit nicely into specially made boxes. They also fit into plastic pages designed to hold 20 of either holder. The pages are transparent and will fit into most loose-leaf binders. It is important to remember not to place coins loose in the pages, as they are often of PVC plastic. Moreover, some of the thumb-cuts made to help remove the coins are large enough for some coins to fall through.

Many specialized coin folders and albums are designed not only to store and exhibit a collection, but to guide collectors. Each coin in the series is individually labeled, making the holder very convenient. It is widely believed that one of the main reasons coin collecting was able to catch on with the

American middle class in the 1930s is the invention of the "penny board," a one-sheet predecessor of these modern coin folders and albums.

Old folders and albums are made by different processes than present ones. Older ones contained substances in the cardboard that tone the coins, although actual corrosion is rare. Today, most manufacturers omit these materials from their albums.

The toning also occurs with the long-term use of the orange-brown two-inch coin envelopes, although it is less of a problem with those of other colors. The toning in this case is caused by sulfur in the paper.

It is best to store a coin collection in a cool, dry environment. Of course, not everyone lives in such a climate. One common answer to this is to store a packet of silica gel in the same container as the coin collection. The gel is a desiccant and will absorb the moisture from the air. It can sometimes be obtained at photo shops, if not as easily through your local coin dealer.

COIN ERRORS

An error is a coin manufactured incorrectly or one that is manufactured correctly on damaged or incorrectly made dies. Errors have been produced by by a wide variety of mistakes, from the wrong metal being used, to the coin being struck off center. The mint tries to prevent such coins from getting out and are usually caught and melted.

1863 Indian Head Cent Struck Off Center

Because the modern automated manufacturing process creates far fewer errors and greater uniformity than in ancient times, collectors of modern coins actually prize such mistakes. (Similar errors may actually reduce the value of ancient coins.) Errors in larger coins, proofs, and commemoratives tend to be scarcer because more attention is paid to the inspection process. Over the last 50 years, more have been getting out than in the past, and as a result, recent errors are not as valuable as early ones.

How each basic type of error occurs is explained following, along with what a typical example of such an error would retail for. Prices are for coins struck within the last 30 years. Coins may be worth more or less depending on the extent of the error. Values for most popular doubled-die cents appear in the regular listings.

Known Counterfeits: Most major doubled-die cents have been counterfeited. Virtually all examples of 1943 copper and 1944 steel cents are counterfeit. A magnet test will reveal deceptive plating, but not cleverly altered dates. Also, it is very easy to cause apparent errors by striking a coin with a coin or hammering foreign matter into it. Apparent off-metal strikes can simply be a coin plated after it was released from the mint. Some very thin coins have been bathed in acid. (Is the surface abraded?) Clipped coins are easily confused for clip errors. Almost all two-headed American coins are concoctions. Do not presume a coin is a mint error until you determine how it was made. There are thousands of such "hoax coins" out there.

Some illustrations here are of foreign coins in order to best show the effects of these errors.

(All values for error coins are for EF to MS-60 condition)

BIE Cent—A special kind of die chip in which a small chip out of the die between B and E in liberty looks like an extra letter I. Fairly common in the 1950s. ....**.25**

Blank—A blank, or planchet, is the piece of metal on which a coin is struck. Sometimes they escape the mint with no processing whatsoever. Other times they escape unstruck, but do make it through the machine that upsets the edge slightly. These are called type I and type II blanks respectively.

Cent	.50
Nickel	2.50
Dime	2.00
Quarter	4.00
Half	12.00
Dollar	30.00

Brockage—Coin struck with a coin and a die instead of two dies. Caused by the previous coin adhering to one die. If it covers the whole die, it creates a "full brockage."

Cent	13.50
Nickel	35.00
Dime	45.00
Quarter	45.00
Half	250.00
Dollar	250.00

Clashed Dies—Coin struck with a die that has been previously struck by another die, leaving some of its impression behind. On the coin, the image of the primary die will be bold, and the image of the residual impression will be very faint.

Cent	.75
Nickel	1.00
Dime	1.75
Quarter	5.50

Half **17.00**

Dollar **18.00**

Clip (2 types)—Coin struck on a blank that has part of its edge missing. There are two causes. A regular clip is caused by the punching device attempting to cut out the form of another coin before a previously punched blank is out of the way. A straight clip is caused when a blank is punched out from too near to the end of the sheet of metal.

Cent .... **.50**

Nickel **2.50**

Dime **2.00**

Quarter **2.50**

Half **10.00**

Dollar **22.00**

Cud—A cud is a raised area of a coin near its edge. It is caused by a piece of the die chipping away. There is no striking surface in that spot to force the coin's metal down.

Cent **1.00**

Nickel **3.00**

Dime **3.50**

Quarter **6.50**

Half **22.00**

Dollar **35.00**

Die Chip—A die chip is similar to a cud, but it can be very small and occur anywhere in the die, not just the edge.

Cent... .25 to 1.00

Nickel .... .25 to 3.00

Dime .... .50 to 3.00

Quarter.. **2.00 to 6.00**

Half .... **5.00 to 20.00**

Dollar .... **5.00 to 30.00**

19??P Susan B. Anthony Dollar
with Cuds Caused by Major Die Breaks

Die Crack—A crack in the die will cause a very fine raised
line across the surface of the coin it strikes. Larger cracks
are worth more than values listed.

Cent.. .50

Nickel .... .75

Dime .... .75

Quarter.. **1.50**

Half **2.50**

Dollar **6.00**

Doubled Die—Caused by several reasons, all in the die manufacturing process. The coins will appear blurred at first glance, but upon inspection, the details will be seen to be doubled.

Prices vary widely, from $10 to $500 or more.

This 1955 Doubled Die Lincoln Cent Is
Worth up to $1,500 in Circulated Grades

Double Struck—When a coin that has been struck fails to eject from between the pair of dies, it will receive a second impression, usually not centered.

Cent	10.00
Nickel	12.00
Dime	12.00
Quarter	40.00
Half	135.00
Dollar	400.00

1886 Double Struck Indian Head Cent

Lamination—Occasionally called an "Occluded Gas Lamination," this error is caused by improper mixture of metal when the alloy is being made. It will appear as flaking on the surface.

Cent	.50
Nickel	3.00
Dime	4.00
Quarter	7.00
Half	12.00
Dollar	25.00

Mismatched Dies—This occurs when one of the two dies is that intended for another coin. To date, all but one has been struck on a blank intended for the larger coin.

Cent and Dime	*two known*
Dollar and Quarter	47,500.00

Off Center—When the blank is not lined up with the dies, only part of the impression is made. The other part of the blank remains just that—blank!

Cent..**1.00**

Nickel **2.50**

Dime **3.00**

Quarter...**8.00**

Half..**30.00**

Dollar..**40.00**

1904 Indian Head Cent Struck Off Center

Struck Through—A coin that had foreign matter on the blank, which was impressed into the surface by thedie.

Cent..**1.50**

Nickel **1.50**

Dime **1.50**

Quarter...**3.50**

Half..**9.00**

Dollar..**11.00**

New York Statehood Quarter Struck on a Dime Planchet

Wrong Metal—When a blank intended for one coin is
accidentally mixed into blanks destined for another and is
struck with those dies.

Cent	**100.00**
Nickel	**40.00**
Dime	**40.00**
Quarter	**45.00**
Half	**125.00**
Dollar	**375.00**

Regular Mint Issues

When the United States was created by the Constitution in 1789 (signed 1787), it was not a given that the nation would have a mint, or even a national coinage. Many were opposed to the idea of government involvement in these matters, and some who weren't thought contracting the manufacture of coinage would be adequate. Even Washington had problems with the original coinage bill, which called for his own name and portrait to appear on each coin. After much protest, the first coinage law of April 2, 1792, replaced Washington with Liberty. This law set up the basic pattern of American coinage still in use today.

HALF CENTS

The half cent is far more popular today than it was when it actually circulated. While half cents permitted very precise dealings in commerce, they were considered a nuisance by those who had to spend them. Demand for them was very slight, mintages were low, and in some years, none were struck for circulation at all. They were so low a priority that the mint sometimes allocated no blanks for them, but struck them on second-hand merchant tokens instead. Even the banks didn't want them. From July 1811 until 1825, none were struck because of pressure from the banking industry. The half cent was finally abandoned in 1857.

Though not as popularly collected as the large cent, they are today considered scarce and desirable coins. Like the large cent, half cents are collected by die variety. Rare die combinations can be worth much more than common ones of the same year. Metal detector finds exhibiting porous surfaces are worth substantially less than the prices listed. Early dates are difficult to find in better than well-worn condition. The Classic Head is much easier to find well preserved.

Known Counterfeits: Cheap cast replicas of the 1793 exist, as do more dangerous counterfeits of that and the 1796 "no pole" variety. Authentic half cents exist with their dates skillfully altered to resemble the rare 1831 date. The 1840s proof restrikes were actually struck by the U.S. mint in the 1850s and 1860s.

Classic Head Type	VG	VF
1809	65.00	85.00
1810	65.00	175.00
1811	225.00	1,250.00
1825	65.00	85.00
1826	65.00	85.00
1828	65.00	85.00
1829	65.00	85.00
1831	3,000.00	7,000.00
1831 restrike	unc.	6,000.00

1825 Half Cent with Classic Head

Classic Head Type	VG	VF
1832	65.00	85.00
1833	65.00	85.00
1834	65.00	85.00
1835	65.00	85.00
1836 proof only	—	5,000.00
1836 restrike proof only	—	18,000.00

Braided Hair Type	VG	VF
1840 proof only	—	4,800.00
1840 restrike proof only	—	4,200.00
1841 proof only	—	4,800.00
1841 restrike proof only	—	4,000.00
1842 proof only	—	4,800.00
1842 restrike proof only	—	4,200.00
1843 proof only	—	4,800.00
1843 restrike proof only	—	4,200.00
1844 proof only	—	4,800.00
1844 restrike proof only	—	4,200.00
1845 proof only	—	4,800.00

Braided Hair Type	VG	VF
1845 restrike proof only	—	4,200.00
1846 proof only	—	4,800.00
1846 restrike proof only	—	4,200.00
1847 proof only	—	4,800.00
1847 restrike proof only	—	4,200.00
1848 proof only	—	4,800.00
1848 restrike proof only	—	4,200.00
1849 proof only	—	4,800.00
1849 restrike proof only	—	4,200.00
1849 large date	60.00	85.00
1850	60.00	85.00
1851	60.00	85.00
1852 proof only	—	60,000.00
1852 restrike proof only	—	4,500.00
1853	60.00	85.00
1854	60.00	85.00
1855	60.00	85.00
1856	60.00	85.00
1857	60.00	85.00

LARGE CENTS

The United States large cent was a result of dual desires, one for a decimal coin worth one-hundredth of a dollar. The other was the need for a coin to replace British halfpennies and their imitations, which had been common in the American colonies. It was slightly larger than the halfpenny, and the concept of decimal coinage was so innovative that the fraction "1/100" had to be written on the coin, along with the edge inscription "ONE HUNDRED FOR A DOLLAR."

The dies for striking early American coins had to be engraved by hand, and no two were identical. Because of this, it has been very popular to collect them, especially the large cents, by die combination.

It is interesting to note that low mintages and mediocre acceptance by the public resulted in the very first large cents being little more than local Philadelphia coinage. Metal was in such short supply that junked copper hardware of inconsistent alloy was used for some early cents, giving a poor quality blank on which to strike the coin. People also resented the chain on the first design of 1793 as a symbol antithetical to liberty, and laughed at the frightened expression they perceived on the face of Miss Liberty.

Later, the coins became so popular that they were considered good luck. In the early 1800s, they were nailed to the rafters of new houses to bring good luck to its inhabitants. These old relics, found with characteristic square nail holes through them, have been given the nickname "rafter cents." While they have discounted value, they still hold historical interest for collectors. Other large cents were stamped or hand engraved with advertising, personal initials, or risqué comments, then placed back into circulation.

During the 1850s, public irritation with the heaviness of the cent began to grow and, after eight years of research into smaller alternatives, the large cent was abandoned in 1857.

Because the hand-engraved dies with which these coins were struck have been individually identified, large cents are very actively collected by die variety. Rare die combinations can be worth much more than common ones of the same year. Metal detector finds exhibiting porous surfaces are worth substantially less than the prices listed. Early dates are particularly difficult to find in better than well-worn condition.

Known Counterfeits: Large cents were not frequently counterfeited in their day. A few rarer dates were later counterfeited by casting (and possibly striking) to fool collectors. They include 1799, 1803, 1805 over 5, and 1851 over inverted 18. 1799 is also known altered from 1798. Some crude museum-souvenirs have been made of Chain Cents as well.

Coronet Type	VG	VF
1816	25.00	84.00
1817 13 stars	25.00	65.00
1817 15 stars	25.00	125.00
1818	25.00	60.00
1819	25.00	63.00
1820	25.00	63.00
1821	40.00	400.00
1822	25.00	90.00
1823	110.00	675.00
1823 restrike	400.00	500.00
1824	25.00	145.00
1825	25.00	110.00
1826	25.00	84.00
1827	25.00	75.00
1828	25.00	84.00
1829	25.00	100.00
1830	25.00	70.00
1831	25.00	63.00
1832	25.00	63.00

Coronet Type	VG	VF
1833	25.00	60.00
1834	25.00	60.00
1835	25.00	56.00
1836	25.00	60.00
1837	25.00	51.00
1838	25.00	51.00
1839	25.00	51.00
1840	25.00	39.00
1841	25.00	45.00
1842	25.00	39.00
1843	25.00	39.00
1844	25.00	39.00
1845	25.00	39.00
1846	25.00	39.00
1847	25.00	39.00
1848	25.00	39.00
1849	25.00	39.00
1850	25.00	39.00
1851	25.00	39.00

Coronet Type	VG	VF
1852	25.00	39.00
1853	25.00	39.00
1854	25.00	39.00
1855	25.00	39.00
1856	25.00	39.00
1857	55.00	85.00

1828 Large Cent with Coronet

1840 Large Cent with Coronet

FLYING EAGLE CENTS

After years of experimenting, the mint introduced its new small cent in 1857. It was less than half the weight of the large cent and was brown to beige in color due to its alloy of 88 percent copper and 12 percent nickel. It depicted an eagle flying left modeled after "Old Pete," a bird that years earlier had served as a mascot at the mint. Initially these were released in certain quantities at *below face value* to encourage their acceptance, but the old large cents were so bulky that people didn't take long to convince. It's interesting to observe, in today's health-conscious society, that the wreath on the reverse contains, among other plants, tobacco.

The 1856 is technically a pattern but was widely distributed at the time, and is generally collected as part of the series.

Known Counterfeits: Most of the 1856 cents encountered are counterfeit. They are usually made from authentic coins with the dates re-engraved.

	VG	VF
1856	7,000.00	8,500.00
1857	24.00	44.00
1858 large letters	24.00	45.00
1858 small letters	24.00	44.00

1858 Flying Eagle Cent

INDIAN HEAD CENTS

The story of the origin of the Indian Head cent is one of the most charming in the field of numismatics. According to legend, James B. Longacre, engraver at the U.S. mint, was entertaining an Indian chief who happened to be wearing his full war bonnet. As a gesture of whimsy, the chief removed his bonnet and placed it on the head of Longacre's little girl, Sarah. According to the story, the engraver instantly perceived that this was the image destined for the next American cent. Admittedly, fewer people believe the tale as time goes on, but it does add a quaint bit of sentimentality to the origin of one of America's favorite coin designs.

When the Indian Head cent was first released, it was struck in the same copper-nickel alloy as the Flying Eagle cent. The reverse was a simple laurel wreath encircling the words ONE CENT. The following year, this was replaced by one of oak, often considered a symbol of authority, into the bottom of which was tied a bundle of arrows. Its top was open enough to fit a small American shield.

In 1864, nickel was removed from the alloy, giving the coin the bronze appearance that has since characterized the U.S. cent. It was also made thinner like our modern cent. This new bronze cent was reminiscent of the private one-cent "Civil War Tokens," which were circulating at the time, and which cost a fraction of a cent to manufacture. The mint was well aware of this obvious savings.

Known Counterfeits: Struck counterfeits of 1867, 1868, 1873 open 3, and 1877 exist. Counterfeit 1908-S and 1909-S are often made by altering real 1908 and 1909 Indian cents.

1882 Bronze Indian Head Cent

Copper-Nickel Alloy	F	XF
1859	20.00	100.00
1860	16.00	53.00
1861	40.00	90.00
1862	10.00	25.00
1863	10.00	25.00
1864	33.00	70.00

Bronze	F	XF
1864	20.00	60.00
1864 "L" on ribbon	125.00	250.00
1865	18.00	35.00
1866	60.00	175.00
1867	70.00	175.00
1868	50.00	160.00
1869	215.00	375.00
1870	200.00	375.00
1871	250.00	380.00
1872	230.00	400.00
1873	50.00	150.00
1873	50.00	150.00

Bronze	F	XF
1874	32.00	95.00
1875	45.00	95.00
1876	60.00	200.00
1877	1,100.00	1,900.00
1878	60.00	210.00
1879	14.00	65.00
1880	6.00	25.00
1881	6.00	18.00
1882	6.00	18.00
1883	5.00	17.50
1884	7.00	25.00
1885	12.00	55.00
1886	18.00	120.00
1887	3.50	18.00
1888	4.00	20.00
1889	3.00	10.00
1890	3.00	10.00
1891	3.00	10.00
1892	3.75	12.00

Bronze	F	XF
1893	3.25	10.00
1894	9.00	42.50
1895	3.25	13.50
1896	2.75	12.00
1897	2.50	10.00
1898	2.75	10.00
1899	2.30	11.00
1900	2.50	12.50
1901	2.00	8.00
1902	2.00	8.00
1903	2.00	8.00
1904	2.00	8.00
1905	2.00	8.00
1906	1.85	8.00
1907	1.85	7.50
1908	2.25	8.00
1908S	75.00	150.00
1909	4.00	17.50
1909S	400.00	525.00

1902 Bronze Indian Head Cent

LINCOLN CENTS

The Lincoln cent was the first regular issue U.S. coin to bear the portrait of a real person. It made its debut to celebrate the one-hundredth year of Lincoln's birth. It was designed by Victor David Brenner, a sculptor from outside the mint's staff. His initials are found prominently on the very first examples to be released. Some thought they were featured too prominently, and the outcry forced their removal, causing two varieties for the first year. Later in 1918, they were added more discreetly under the truncation of the shoulder.

Lincoln cents were a bronze alloy of 95 percent copper until 1943, when they were changed to zinc-coated steel to save copper for the war effort. Because some of them were confused with dimes, they were replaced in 1944 and 1945 with cents made from melted spent shell casings, resulting in a much more conventional appearance.

The original alloy was restored from 1946 until 1982, when it was finally abandoned for zinc plated with copper. This was to reduce the expense of manufacturing the cent. Many people don't realize it, but if you cut one of the cents struck today in half, it will not be orange or brown inside but white, revealing its true composition.

A new reverse was introduced in 1959 for the 150th anniversary of Lincoln's birth and the 50th anniversary of the Lincoln cent. Still in use today, it depicts the Lincoln Memorial in Washington D.C.

The Lincoln cent is one of the most popularly collected coins on earth. It is collected in most grades, and even the rarities can be found without too long a search.

Known Counterfeits: The 1909S VDB, 1909S, 1914D, 1922-Plain, 1931S, and 1955 doubled dies have been extensively counterfeited. Most are altered cents of other dates. Counterfeits also exist of the 1972 doubled die. Virtually all 1943 bronze and 1944 steel cents are counterfeit. A magnet test will reveal the crudest counterfeits made by plating. Other 1943 bronze have been made by altering 1948 and by striking with false dies.

In addition to counterfeits, the collector should be aware of "reprocessed" cents. These are circulated 1943 steel cents given a fresh zinc coating to make them appear uncirculated. Many hobbyists are quite willing to have them in their collections, but it is important to know the difference. Don't look for luster, but rather for traces of flatness at the cheekbone.

1909S VDB Lincoln Cent with Wheat Ears Reverse

Wheat Ears Reverse	VF	MS-60
1909 VDB	5.00	9.50
1909S VDB	750.00	1,250.00
1909	2.00	13.50
1909S	135.00	260.00
1910	.60	14.50
1910S	14.00	62.50
1911	1.35	18.00
1911D	13.50	80.00
1911S	25.00	150.00
1912	5.00	30.00
1912D	20.00	140.00
1912S	20.00	120.00
1913	3.50	28.00
1913D	8.50	90.00
1913S	12.00	135.00
1914	4.00	40.00
1914D	300.00	1,400.00
1914S	25.00	250.00
1915	10.00	80.00

Wheat Ears Reverse	VF	MS-60
1915D	5.00	50.00
1915S	13.50	150.00
1916	1.80	14.00
1916D	3.50	60.00
1916S	3.50	68.00
1917	1.50	13.00
1917D	3.00	58.00
1917S	2.25	58.00
1918	1.00	12.00
1918D	2.50	60.00
1918S	2.25	60.00
1919	.75	9.00
1919D	2.20	50.00
1919S	1.70	36.00
1920	.75	12.00
1920D	2.50	55.00
1920S	2.00	80.00
1921	1.75	36.00
1921S	4.00	90.00

1922 Plain (No D) Lincoln Cent with Wheat Ears Reverse

Wheat Ears Reverse	VF	MS-60
1922D	15.00	75.00
1922 plain	1,150.00	6,800.00
1923	1.25	12.00
1923S	5.50	185.00
1924	1.25	20.00
1924D	30.00	235.00
1924S	3.00	95.00
1925	1.00	10.00
1925D	2.00	50.00
1925S	1.50	60.00
1926	.80	8.00
1926D	1.50	60.00
1926S	7.00	110.00
1927	.80	8.00
1927D	1.25	55.00
1927S	3.50	65.00
1928	.80	8.50
1928D	1.50	30.00
1928S	2.20	65.00

Wheat Ears Reverse	VF	MS-60
1929	.80	6.00
1929D	1.50	18.00
1929S	1.50	16.00
1930	.50	4.00
1930D	.75	12.00
1930S	.80	10.00
1931	1.40	17.50
1931D	5.00	52.00
1931S	75.00	100.00
1932	3.00	18.50
1932D	2.00	16.00
1933	2.20	17.00
1933D	3.50	18.00
1934	.25	4.00
1934D	.45	16.50
1935	.25	2.50
1935D	.30	5.50
1935S	.40	12.00
1936	.25	2.00

1932D Lincoln Cent with Wheat Ears Reverse

Wheat Ears Reverse	VF	MS-60
1936D	.25	2.75
1936S	.35	2.75
1937	.20	1.75
1937D	.25	2.50
1937S	.25	3.00
1938	.20	2.00
1938D	.45	2.70
1938S	.70	2.80
1939	.20	1.00
1939D	.60	2.25
1939S	.25	1.35
1940	.25	.95
1940D	.25	1.00
1940S	.25	1.25
1941	.15	.85
1941D	.20	2.00
1941S	.20	2.25
1942	.15	.50
1942D	.15	.50

*1943 Lincoln cents were produced
with a zinc-coated steel during WWII.*

Wheat Ears Reverse	VF	MS-60
1942S	.20	3.50
1943 steel	.30	.85
1943D steel	.35	1.00
1943S steel	.40	2.50
1944	.15	.50
1944D	.15	.45
1944 D over S	120.00	375.00
1944S	.15	.45
1945	.15	.60
1945D	.15	.70
1945S	.15	.45
1946	.15	.35
1946D	.15	.50
1946S	.15	.50
1947	.15	.60
1947D	.15	.40
1947S	.15	.55
1948	.15	.50
1948D	.15	.45

Wheat Ears Reverse	VF	MS-60
1948S	.15	.65
1949	.15	.75
1949D	.15	.50
1949S	.15	1.00
1950	.15	.50
1950D	.15	.50
1950S	.15	.80
1951	.15	.90
1951D	.15	.50
1951S	.15	.75
1952	.15	.50
1952D	.15	.50
1952S	.15	1.00
1953	.15	.50
1953D	.15	.50
1953S	.15	.45
1954	.15	.75
1954D	.15	.35
1954S	.15	.35

Wheat Ears Reverse	VF	MS-60
1955	.15	.30
1955 doubled die	950.00	1,550.00
1955 minor date shift or "poor man's doubled die"	.15	1.00
1955D	.15	.30
1955S	.15	.60
1956	.15	.30
1956D	.15	.30
1957	.15	.30
1957D	.15	.30
1958	.15	.30
1958D	.15	.30

Lincoln Memorial Reverse	BU
1959	.20
1959D	.30
1960 large date	.20
1960 small date	2.50
1960D large date	.30
1960D small date	.30
1961	.20
1961D	.20
1962	.20
1962D	.20
1963	.20
1963D	.20
1964	.20
1964D	.20
1965	.20
1966	.20
1967	.20
1968	.20
1968D	.20

Lincoln Memorial Reverse	BU
1968S	.20
1969	.40
1969D	.20
1969S	.20
1970	.20
1970D	.20
1970S small date	30.00
1970S large date	.20
1971	.20
1971D	.25
1971S	.35
1972	.15
1972 doubled die	400.00
1972D	.15
1972S	.15
1973	.15
1973D	.15
1973S	.15
1974	.15

Lincoln Memorial Reverse	BU
1974D	.15
1974S	.15
1975	.15
1975D	.15
1975S proof only	5.50
1976	.15
1976D	.15
1976S proof only	5.00
1977	.15
1977D	.15
1977S proof only	3.00
1978	.15
1978D	.15
1978S proof only	3.00
1979	.15
1979D	.15
1979S proof only	4.00
1980	.15
1980D	.15

1982S Lincoln Cent with Lincoln Memorial Reverse

Lincoln Memorial Reverse	BU
1980S proof only	2.25
1981	.15
1981D	.15
1981S proof only	3.00
1982	.15
1982D	.15
1982S proof only	3.00

Copper Plated Zinc	BU
1982	.20
1982D	.15
1983	.15
1983 doubled die rev.	300.00
1983D	.15
1983S proof only	4.00
1984	.15
1984 doubled die	200.00
1984D	.30
1984S proof only	4.50

Copper Plated Zinc	BU
1985	.15
1985D	.15
1985S proof only	5.00
1986	.30
1986D	.15
1986S proof only	7.50
1987	.15
1987D	.15
1987S proof only	5.00
1988	.15
1988D	.15
1988S proof only	8.00
1989	.15
1989D	.15
1989S proof only	3.00
1990	.15
1990D	.15
1990S proof only	5.75
1990S w/o S *proof only*	3,000.00

1990S Proof Lincoln Cent Error
(Coin Struck at San Francisco Mint without S Mark)

Copper Plated Zinc	BU
1991	.15
1991D	.15
1991S proof only	20.00

Copper Plated Zinc	BU
1992	.15
1992D	.15
1992S proof only	6.50
1993	.15
1993D	.15
1993S proof only	9.50
1994	.15
1994D	.15
1994S proof only	8.50
1995	.15
1995 doubled die	25.00
1995D	.15
1995S proof only	9.50
1996	.15
1996D	.15
1996S proof only	6.50
1997	.15
1997D	.15
1997S proof only	10.50
1998	.15

Copper Plated Zinc	BU
1998D	.15
1998S proof only	9.50
1999	.15
1999D	.15
1999S proof only	6.00
2000	.15
2000D	.15
2000S proof only	5.00
2001	.15
2001D	.15
2001S proof only	5.00
2002	.15
2002D	.15
2002S proof only	5.00
2003	.15
2003D	.15
2003S proof only	5.00
2004	.15
2004D	.15
2004S proof only	5.00

TWO-CENT PIECES

Throughout the Civil War, people hoarded coins, preferring to spend the less valuable private tokens and small denomination paper money then available. If the North fell, they thought that at least real coins would retain some value. A shortage of small change resulted. The two-cent piece was introduced in an attempt to alleviate this shortage. It was the first coin to carry the inscription "In God We Trust."

These are usually found well worn, with fewer than one in one hundred surviving in Fine or better condition.

Known Counterfeits: Counterfeits are not particularly common, though some scarce die-struck ones are known.

	F	XF
1864 small motto (open D in God)	200.00	550.00
1864 large motto (narrow D in God)	18.00	37.00
1865	18.00	37.00
1866	19.00	37.00
1867	20.00	38.00
1868	30.00	48.00
1869	30.00	53.00

	F	XF
1870	35.00	90.00
1871	40.00	110.00
1872	400.00	760.00
1873 closed 3 proof only	—	2,000.00
1873 open 3 proof restrike	—	2,200.00

1867 Two-Cent Piece

SILVER THREE-CENT PIECES

Different times have different priorities, and the reasons for striking coins in one era don't always seem to make sense to the people living in another. This is the case of the silver three-cent piece, often called the "trime." It and the three-dollar gold piece were issued to make it easier to purchase single and sheets of three-cent, first-class postage stamps. Despite the extreme awkwardness of their small size, they were accepted enough in commerce that they continued to be struck in significant quantities for 12 years.

Its thinness prevented it from striking well, and the mint attempted to modify its design repeatedly. Obtaining a fully struck coin with no weak spots, even in higher grades is truly difficult. Another problem resulting from its thinness was its frequent bending, dents, and crinkling. Prices given are for flat, undamaged examples.

Known Counterfeits: Counterfeits made to pass in circulation were struck in base silver and white metal for early dates, German silver (copper-nickel-zinc) dated 1860 and 1861. A struck counterfeit also exists for 1864.

1863 Silver Three-Cent Piece with Double Border Around Star

No Border Around Star	F	XF
1851	30.00	65.00
1851O	40.00	130.00
1852	30.00	65.00
1853	30.00	65.00

Triple Border Around Star	F	XF
1854	30.00	95.00
1855	55.00	165.00
1856	30.00	90.00

Triple Border Around Star	F	XF
1857	30.00	90.00
1858	30.00	90.00

Double Border Around Star	F	XF
1859	30.00	65.00
1860	30.00	68.00
1861	30.00	65.00
1862	30.00	65.00
1863	350.00	400.00
1864	350.00	400.00
1865	400.00	465.00
1866	350.00	400.00
1867	400.00	465.00
1868	400.00	465.00
1869	400.00	465.00
1870	400.00	465.00
1871	410.00	465.00
1872	430.00	500.00
1873 proof only	—	1,750.00

NICKEL THREE-CENT PIECES

The fact that the tiny silver three-cent piece survived at all indicated that there was some usefulness to that denomination, but its size was impractical. With silver being hoarded during the Civil War, the need for a convenient non-silver coin of this value was even more apparent. The three-cent coin was thus made bigger and changed to an alloy of 75 percent copper and 25 percent nickel, just enough nickel to give it a white color. Despite their active use in commerce for decades, they are not difficult to find well preserved.

Known Counterfeits: Few if any counterfeits of this coin are known.

	F	XF
1865	16.00	27.00
1866	16.00	27.00
1867	16.00	27.00
1868	16.00	27.00
1869	16.00	27.00
1870	16.50	28.00
1871	16.00	29.00
1872	16.50	27.00
1873	16.00	30.00

1865 Nickel Three-Cent Piece

	F	XF
1874	16.00	27.00
1875	16.00	33.00
1876	17.00	38.00
1877 proof only	—	2,550.00
1878 proof only	—	900.00
1879	77.00	95.00
1880	100.00	135.00
1881	16.00	27.00
1882	92.00	115.00
1883	200.00	280.00
1884	475.00	500.00
1885	550.00	600.00
1886 proof only	—	575.00
1887	275.00	325.00
1888	50.00	70.00
1889	100.00	120.00

LIBERTY NICKELS

The Liberty nickel had one of the most controversial beginnings of all American coins. The original design had the denomination of five cents indicated simply by the Roman numeral V, with the word cents simply understood. Or so the mint expected. However, some unprincipled persons gold plated these coins and passed them off as the new five-dollar coin. These plated frauds became known as racketeer nickels and prompted an immediate change in the coin's design. The word "cents" was added boldly underneath the large V.

Today, racketeer nickels have some value as collector's novelties, but not as much as a natural, unaltered coin. Interestingly, the original "no cents" nickel is quite common today in medium to high grades, perhaps as an evidence of it being considered a novelty in its day.

The famous 1913 Liberty nickel is not an authorized mint issue, but was struck at the U.S. mint by a scheming employee with an eye to profit. Carefully marketed, the first advertisements to purchase these rare coins were placed by the original seller, knowing that no one else had any to sell, but knowing that this would excite interest in the numismatic community. Today, it is one of the most valuable coins in the world!

Known Counterfeits: There are counterfeits of the 1913, but they are somewhat less dangerous, as all five extant pieces are in known hands. 1912S pieces exist made from altered 1912D nickels.

1896 Liberty Nickel

	F	XF
1883 no cents	7.00	9.00
1883 with cents	25.00	65.00
1884	27.50	70.00
1885	700.00	950.00
1886	340.00	575.00
1887	27.00	60.00
1888	45.00	125.00
1889	22.00	52.00
1890	23.00	56.00
1891	16.00	52.00
1892	17.50	58.00
1893	17.50	46.00
1894	80.00	190.00
1895	22.00	60.00
1896	30.00	68.00
1897	10.50	36.00
1898	9.50	33.00
1899	6.75	30.00
1900	6.75	30.00

1907 Liberty Nickel

	F	XF
1901	6.50	27.50
1902	4.50	27.50
1903	4.50	27.50
1904	4.50	28.50
1905	4.25	27.50
1906	4.00	27.50
1907	4.00	27.50
1908	4.00	27.50
1909	4.50	30.00
1910	4.00	25.00
1911	4.00	25.00
1912	4.00	25.00
1912D	7.00	65.00
1912S	225.00	750.00
1913 proof	—	3,000,000.00

BUFFALO NICKELS

The Buffalo Nickel, also called the Indian Head nickel, was one of the most artistically progressive American coins to have been struck when first issued. It was designed by James Earl Fraser, a noted sculptor of the era. Traditional belief holds that three different Indians posed for the obverse portrait, but this theory has recently been called into question.

The original reverse depicting an American bison standing on a mound was changed for practical reasons the year it was issued, as the words FIVE CENTS were in such high relief that they would quickly wear off. The second reverse has the denomination in a recess below a plane on which the bison stands. The date is rendered in high relief on these coins as well, and below Very Good usually wears off. Such dateless coins are of little value.

One entertaining sidelight to the Buffalo nickel is the Hobo nickel. This relic of American folk art consists of a Buffalo nickel with the portrait re-engraved by hand into a variety of different portraits. It was some individuals' way of fighting the poverty of the Great Depression, by making these works of art and selling them at a modest profit. Over the last few years they have come into their own, and attempts to identify individual artists have met with some success.

Known Counterfeits: The most famous counterfeit in the series is that of the Three-Legged Buffalo variety of 1937D. It should be noted that a real three-legged buffalo can be distinguished not simply because of its missing leg, but based on numerous minor details being missing where the design meets the field. Other counterfeits are coins altered to appear to be 1913S Type II, 1918/7D, 1921S, 1924S, 1926D, and 1926S.

1913D Buffalo Nickel

	F	Unc.
1913 mound	10.00	32.00
1913D mound	19.00	60.00
1913S mound	50.00	110.00
1913 plain	9.50	32.50
1913D plain	135.00	250.00
1913S plain	375.00	550.00
1914	19.00	45.00
1914D	120.00	360.00
1914S	42.00	150.00
1915	7.00	48.00
1915D	33.00	225.00
1915S	75.00	550.00
1916	5.50	41.00
1916D	21.00	150.00
1916S	16.00	165.00
1917	5.50	55.00
1917D	35.00	315.00
1917S	65.00	365.00
1918	5.50	95.00
1918 8 over 7	2,700.00	28,500.00

	F	Unc.
1918D	41.00	410.00
1918S	45.00	500.00
1919	2.50	45.00
1919D	55.00	540.00
1919S	45.00	510.00
1920	2.50	50.00
1920D	27.00	535.00
1920S	20.00	500.00
1921	6.75	115.00
1921S	185.00	1,500.00
1923	3.00	55.00
1923S	19.00	460.00
1924	4.00	68.00
1924D	27.50	335.00
1924S	96.00	2,250.00
1925	3.50	40.00
1925D	40.00	350.00
1925S	17.50	385.00
1926	2.25	35.00
1926D	24.00	285.00

1924 Buffalo Nickel

	F	Unc.
1926S	78.00	4,500.00
1927	2.25	30.00
1927D	8.00	160.00
1927S	5.00	480.00
1928	2.25	35.00
1928D	4.00	59.00
1928S	2.25	200.00
1929	2.25	35.00
1929D	2.25	55.00
1929S	2.00	45.00
1930	2.25	29.00
1930S	2.25	43.00
1931S	16.00	45.00
1934	2.25	48.00
1934D	2.35	75.00
1935	1.10	19.00
1935D	2.00	67.00
1935S	1.10	49.00
1936	1.00	15.00

1937D "Three-Legged" Buffalo

	F	Unc.
1936D	1.00	34.00
1936S	1.00	34.00
1937	1.00	14.00
1937D	1.00	18.00
1937D 3-legged	700.00	2,300.00
1937S	1.00	24.00
1938D	2.00	17.00
1938D D over S	10.00	45.00

JEFFERSON NICKELS

The Jefferson Nickel was the first circulating U.S. coin to be designed by public contest. Felix Schlag won $1,000 for his design featuring Jefferson's portrait on one side, and his home Monticello on the other. The initial rendition lacks the designer's initials, which were not added until 1966.

Due to the difficulty of getting the metal to flow into every crevice of the die, many coins are struck with the steps of Monticello on the standard reverse incompletely struck. Full step nickels sometimes command a premium from specialists.

During World War II, nickel was needed for the war effort, so from mid-1942 to the end of 1945 "nickels" were struck in an unusual alloy of 56-percent copper, 35-percent silver and 9-percent manganese. These War Nickels bear a large mint mark over the dome. These coins exhibit great brilliance when new, but quickly turn an ugly dull color with a moderate amount of wear.

A pair of special nickels were issued for circulation in 2004, struck to commemorate the bicentennial of the expedition of exploration from St. Louis to the Pacific, led by Meriwether Lewis and William Clark. They bear the standard Jefferson obverse. One reverse bears clasped hands adapted from a Jefferson-era Indian peace medal. The other shows an old keelboat used for navigating rivers.

Known Counterfeits: 1950D. Crude casts were also made to circulate in the 1940s.

1939 Jefferson Nickel

	VF	BU
1938	.80	4.00
1938D	1.25	3.50
1938S	2.00	4.00
1939	.25	1.75
1939D	5.00	38.00
1939S	1.50	15.00
1940	.25	1.00
1940D	.30	1.50
1940S	.25	2.50
1941	.25	1.00
1941D	.30	2.50
1941S	.30	3.75
1942	.25	5.00
1942D	.60	27.00
Wartime Silver Alloy	**VF**	**BU**
1942P	1.00	6.00
1942S	1.10	6.00
1943P	1.00	2.75
1943P 3 over 2	40.00	175.00

Wartime Silver Alloy	VF	BU
1943D	1.50	3.00
1943S	1.00	3.00
1944P	1.00	3.00
1944D	1.00	6.50
1944S	1.25	3.50
1945P	1.00	3.50
1945D	1.00	3.50
1945S	.80	2.60

Regular Alloy	VF	BU
1946	.25	.80
1946D	.25	.85
1946S	.30	.50
1947	.25	.75
1947D	.25	.90
1947S	.25	.80
1948	.25	.50
1948D	.25	1.20
1948S	.25	1.00
1949	.25	1.25

Regular Alloy	VF	BU
1949D	.30	1.00
1949D D over S	40.00	170.00
1949S	.45	1.50
1950	.35	1.50
1950D	6.00	8.50
1951	.40	1.25
1951D	.40	1.45
1951S	.50	1.75
1952	.25	.85
1952D	.30	1.50
1952S	.25	.75
1953	.25	.40
1953D	.25	.40
1953S	.25	.50
1954	.25	.35
1954D	.25	.35
1954S	.25	.50
1954S S over D	9.00	22.00
1955	.40	.75

Regular Alloy	VF	BU
1955D	—	.35
1955D D over S	8.50	33.00
1956	—	.25
1956D	—	.25
1957	—	.25
1957D	—	.25
1958	—	.30
1958D	—	.25
1959	—	.30
1959D	—	.25
1960	—	.25
1960D	—	.25
1961	—	.25
1961D	—	.25
1962	—	.25
1962D	—	.25
1963	—	.25
1963D	—	.25
1964	—	.25

1965 Regular Alloy Jefferson Nickel

Regular Alloy	VF	BU
1964D	—	.25
1965	—	.25
1966	—	.25
1967	—	.25
1968D	—	.25
1968S	—	.25
1969D	—	.25
1969S	—	.25
1970D	—	.25
1970S	—	.25
1971	—	.75
1971D	—	.25
1971S proof only	—	**1.60**
1972	—	.25
1972D	—	.25
1972S proof only	—	**2.00**
1973	—	.25
1973D	—	.25
1973S proof only	—	**1.75**

Regular Alloy	VF	BU
1974	—	.25
1974D	—	.25
1974S proof only	—	**2.00**
1975	—	.25
1975D	—	.25
1975S proof only	—	**2.25**
1976	—	.25
1976D	—	.25
1976S proof only	—	**2.00**
1977	—	.25
1977D	—	.25
1977S proof only	—	**1.75**
1978	—	.25
1978D	—	.25
1978S proof only	—	**1.75**
1979	—	.25
1979D	—	.25
1979S proof only	—	**1.50**
1980P	—	.25
1980D	—	.25

Regular Alloy	VF	BU
1980S proof only	—	**1.50**
1981P	—	**.25**
1981D	—	**.25**
1981S proof only	—	**2.00**
1982P	—	**1.00**
1982D	—	**1.25**
1982S proof only	—	**3.00**
1983P	—	**1.50**
1983D	—	**1.00**
1983S proof only	—	**4.00**
1984P	—	**1.25**
1984D	—	**.25**
1984S proof only	—	**5.00**
1985P	—	**.30**
1985D	—	**.30**
1985S proof only	—	**4.00**
1986P	—	**.30**
1986D	—	**.85**
1986S proof only	—	**7.00**
1987P	—	**.25**

Regular Alloy	VF	BU
1987D	—	.25
1987S proof only	—	3.50
1988P	—	.25
1988D	—	.25
1988S proof only	—	5.50
1989P	—	.25
1989D	—	.25
1989S proof only	—	4.50
1990P	—	.25
1990D	—	.25
1990S proof only	—	5.50
1991P	—	.25
1991D	—	.25
1991S proof only	—	5.00
1992P	—	.75
1992D	—	.25
1992S proof only	—	4.00
1993P	—	.25
1993D	—	4.00
1993S proof only	—	.25

Regular Alloy	VF	BU
1994P	—	.25
1994P matte finish	—	75.00
1994D	—	.25
1994S proof only	—	4.00
1995P	—	.25
1995D	—	.35
1995S proof only	—	6.50
1996P	—	.25
1996D	—	.25
1996S proof only	—	3.00
1997P	—	.25
1997P matte finish	—	200.00
1997D	—	.25
1997S proof only	—	5.00
1998P	—	.25
1998D	—	.25
1998S proof only	—	4.50
1999P	—	.25
1999D	—	.25
1999S proof only	—	3.50

2004 Jefferson Nickel with Lewis and Clark Keelboat Reverse

Regular Alloy	VF	BU
2000P	—	.25
2000D	—	.25
2000S proof only	—	2.00
2001P	—	.30
2001D	—	.30
2001S proof only	—	2.00
2002P	—	.25
2002D	—	.25
2002S proof only	—	2.00
2003P	—	.30
2003D	—	.30
2003S proof only	—	2.00
2004P peace rev.	—	.35
2004D peace rev.	—	.35
2004S peace rev. proof only	—	8.00
2004P keelboat rev.	—	.35
2004D keelboat rev.	—	.35
2004S keelboat rev. proof only	—	8.00
2005P Buffalo rev	—	.35
2005D Buffalo rev.	—	.35

2005 Jefferson Nickel with Buffalo Reverse

SEATED LIBERTY HALF DIMES

Following the introduction of Christian Gobrecht's Seated Liberty design on the silver dollar, smaller coins were gradually brought into harmony with this design. It is generally accepted that the seated goddess version of Liberty was directly or indirectly inspired by depictions of the Roman allegory of Britannia on British coins. The half dime and dime, because of their small size, were redesigned to have a laurel wreath encircling the denomination on the reverse, rather than an eagle.

Several minor changes were introduced over the life of this coin. After only a year, the plain obverse was ornamented by 13 stars. Two years later, additional drapery was added below Liberty's elbow. The arrows by the date from 1853 to 1855 indicate a 7-1/2 percent reduction in weight. A far more obvious design change was the shift of the words UNITED STATES OF AMERICA from the reverse to the obverse in 1860.

The seated half dime's thinness resulted in frequent bending and dents. Prices given are for flat, undamaged examples.

Known Counterfeits: Counterfeit half dimes are not frequently encountered.

1837 Seated Liberty Half Dime with Plain Obverse Field

Seated Liberty— Plain Obverse Field	VG	VF
1837	35.00	100.00
1838O	125.00	400.00

Seated Liberty — Stars On Obverse	VG	VF
1838	19.00	26.00
1839	19.00	29.00
1839O	19.00	35.00
1840	19.00	26.00
1840O	19.00	50.00
1841	19.00	26.00
1841O	19.00	42.00
1842	19.00	26.00
1842O	45.00	225.00
1843	19.00	26.00
1844	19.00	26.00
1844O	105.00	450.00
1845	19.00	26.00
1846	450.00	1,150.00
1847	19.00	26.00
1848	19.00	26.00
1848O	25.00	50.00
1849	19.00	26.00

*1855O Seated Liberty Half Dime with
Stars and Arrows on Obverse*

Seated Liberty — Stars On Obverse	VG	VF
1849O	40.00	225.00
1849 overdates	19.00	40.00
1850	19.00	26.00
1850O	19.00	50.00
1851	19.00	26.00
1851O	19.00	35.00
1852	19.00	26.00
1852O	32.00	135.00
1853 no arrows	36.00	100.00
1853O no arrows	260.00	675.00
1853 arrows	19.00	26.00
1853O arrows	19.00	26.00
1854	19.00	26.00
1854O	19.00	26.00
1855	19.00	26.00
1855O	20.00	55.00
1856	19.00	26.00
1856O	19.00	38.00

1863 Seated Liberty Half Dime with Legend on Obverse

Seated Liberty — Stars On Obverse	VG	VF
1857	19.00	26.00
1857O	19.00	33.00
1858	19.00	26.00
1858O	19.00	36.00
1859	19.00	34.00
1859O	19.00	40.00

Seated Liberty — Legend On Obverse	VG	VF
1860	19.00	26.00
1861	19.00	26.00
1862	19.00	26.00
1863	225.00	375.00
1863S	35.00	75.00
1864	425.00	600.00
1864S	65.00	150.00
1865	400.00	550.00
1865S	35.00	75.00

Seated Liberty — Legend On Obverse	VG	VF
1866	450.00	650.00
1866S	35.00	75.00
1867	550.00	800.00
1867S	35.00	75.00
1868	70.00	170.00
1868S	25.00	40.00
1869	25.00	40.00
1869S	22.00	35.00
1870	22.00	35.00
1870S	unique	
1871	13.00	26.00
1871S	30.00	60.00
1872	13.00	26.00
1872S	13.00	26.00
1873	13.00	26.00
1873S	25.00	40.00

SEATED LIBERTY DIMES

Following the introduction of the Seated Liberty design by Christian Gobrecht on the silver dollar, the smaller coins were gradually brought into harmony with this design. It is generally accepted that the seated goddess version of Liberty was directly or indirectly inspired by depictions of the Roman allegory of Britannia on British coins. The dime and half dime, because of their small size, were redesigned to have a laurel wreath encircling the denomination on the reverse, rather than an eagle.

There were several minor changes over the life of this coin. After somewhat more than a year, the plain obverse was ornamented by 13 stars. A year later, additional drapery was added below Liberty's elbow. The arrows by the date from 1853 to 1855 indicate a 7 percent reduction in weight, those in 1873 to 1874 a minuscule increase. A far more obvious design change was the shift of the words UNITED STATES OF AMERICA from the reverse to the obverse in 1860.

The seated dime's thinness resulted in frequent bending and dents. Prices given are for flat, undamaged examples.

Known Counterfeits: Collector counterfeits of seated dimes are not frequently encountered, but circulating counterfeits were struck in copper, lead, and white metal (tin and lead alloys), particularly during the 1850s-1860s.

Seated Liberty—Obverse Field Plain	VG	VF
1837	40.00	275.00
1838O	45.00	300.00

1844 Seated Liberty Dime with Stars on Obverse

Seated Liberty — Stars On Obverse	VG	VF
1838 (varieties)	18.00	25.00
1839	18.00	35.00
1839O	18.00	45.00
1840	18.00	30.00
1840O	22.00	70.00
1840 extra drapery from elbow	45.00	185.00
1841	18.00	25.00
1841O	18.00	30.00
1842	18.00	23.00
1842O	18.00	75.00
1843	18.00	23.00
1843O	65.00	275.00
1844	350.00	800.00
1845	18.00	23.00
1845O	35.00	200.00
1846	200.00	400.00
1847	25.00	75.00
1848	20.00	45.00
1849	18.00	28.00

Seated Liberty — Stars On Obverse	VG	VF
1849O	30.00	120.00
1850	18.00	25.00
1850O	25.00	70.00
1851	18.00	23.00
1851O	25.00	75.00
1852	18.00	23.00
1852O	30.00	125.00
1853 no arrows	90.00	195.00
1853 arrows	18.00	23.00
1853O arrows	18.00	45.00
1854	18.00	23.00
1854O	18.00	25.00
1855	18.00	23.00
1856	18.00	23.00
1856O	18.00	35.00
1856S	225.00	500.00
1857	18.00	23.00
1857O	18.00	25.00
1858	18.00	35.00

Seated Liberty — Stars On Obverse	VG	VF
1858O	25.00	85.00
1858S	150.00	425.00
1859	20.00	45.00
1859O	20.00	45.00
1859S	200.00	500.00
1860S	40.00	135.00
Seated Liberty— Legend On Obverse	VG	VF
1860	22.00	31.00
1860O	475.00	1,650.00
1861	18.00	23.00
1861S	85.00	275.00
1862	18.00	25.00
1862S	60.00	175.00
1863	450.00	700.00
1863S	40.00	125.00
1864	425.00	650.00
1864S	35.00	95.00
1865	450.00	750.00

Seated Liberty— Legend On Obverse	VG	VF
1865S	45.00	125.00
1866	500.00	800.00
1866S	50.00	145.00
1867	700.00	1,100.00
1867S	50.00	125.00
1868	22.00	40.00
1868S	30.00	80.00
1869	30.00	75.00
1869S	25.00	45.00
1870	22.00	38.00
1870S	350.00	550.00
1871	20.00	33.00
1871CC	1,850.00	4,000.00
1871S	55.00	115.00
1872	18.00	23.00
1872CC	650.00	2,000.00
1872S	60.00	150.00
1873 closed 3	18.00	27.00
1873 open 3	30.00	60.00

1877 Seated Liberty Dime with Legend on Obverse

Seated Liberty—Legend On Obverse	VG	VF
1873CC	Unique	
1873 arrows	18.00	50.00
1873CC arrows	1,850.00	4,000.00
1873S arrows	30.00	70.00
1874 arrows	18.00	50.00
1874CC arrows	5,500.00	12,500.00
1874S arrows	70.00	160.00
1875	18.00	23.00
1875CC	18.00	23.00
1875S	18.00	23.00
1876	18.00	23.00
1876CC	18.00	23.00
1876S	18.00	23.00
1877	18.00	23.00
1877CC	18.00	23.00
1877S	18.00	30.00
1878	18.00	23.00
1878CC	75.00	190.00
1879	250.00	385.00

Seated Liberty— Legend On Obverse	VG	VF
1880	215.00	300.00
1881	225.00	325.00
1882	18.00	23.00
1883	18.00	23.00
1884	18.00	23.00
1884S	35.00	65.00
1885	18.00	23.00
1885S	475.00	1,450.00
1886	18.00	23.00
1886S	55.00	95.00
1887	18.00	23.00
1887S	18.00	23.00
1888	18.00	23.00
1888S	18.00	25.00
1889	18.00	23.00
1889S	18.00	35.00
1890	18.00	23.00
1890S	18.00	50.00
1891	18.00	23.00

Seated Liberty— Legend On Obverse	VG	VF
1891O	18.00	23.00
1891S	18.00	25.00

BARBER DIMES

The dime, quarter, and half dollar introduced in 1892 bear a portrait head of Liberty instead of an entire figure. They were designed by Chief Engraver Charles E. Barber, after whom they have been popularly named. More practical than artistically adventurous, contemporaries thought the design rather boring if not unpleasant. Because of its small size, the dime differed from the other two denominations in the Barber series in that the reverse simply has the value within a wreath, rather than an eagle, much as occurred with the Seated Liberty coinage.

Known Counterfeits: The rare 1894S has certainly been counterfeited.

	F	XF
1892	16.00	24.00
1892O	27.00	50.00
1892S	175.00	245.00
1893, 3 over 2	75.00	275.00

1898S Barber Dime

	F	XF
1893	17.50	35.00
1893O	110.00	150.00
1893S	25.00	55.00
1894	100.00	145.00
1894O	190.00	330.00
1894S	very rare proof	125,000.00
1895	300.00	485.00
1895O	715.00	1,950.00
1895S	120.00	195.00
1896	50.00	83.00
1896O	265.00	400.00
1896S	280.00	345.00
1897	6.50	24.00
1897O	250.00	400.00
1897S	90.00	120.00
1898	6.50	21.50
1898O	80.00	180.00
1898S	26.00	58.00
1899	6.50	20.00
1899O	68.00	125.00

1903S Barber Dime

	F	XF
1899S	19.50	40.00
1900	6.50	21.50
1900O	95.00	200.00
1900S	9.50	23.00
1901	5.75	20.00
1901O	12.00	42.00
1901S	340.00	420.00
1902	4.50	20.00
1902O	13.00	42.50
1902S	52.00	95.00
1903	3.50	20.00
1903O	9.75	26.00
1903S	335.00	800.00
1904	6.00	20.00
1904S	140.00	270.00
1905	4.50	20.00
1905O	30.00	60.00
1905S	6.00	32.00
1906	3.50	20.00
1906D	8.00	29.00

	F	XF
1906O	44.00	85.00
1906S	10.00	39.00
1907	3.50	20.00
1907D	7.50	34.00
1907O	29.00	55.00
1907S	11.00	42.00
1908	3.50	20.00
1908D	5.50	28.00
1908O	42.50	72.00
1908S	9.00	35.00
1909	3.50	20.00
1909D	58.00	115.00
1909O	9.50	28.00
1909S	83.00	165.00
1910	3.50	20.00
1910D	7.75	36.00
1910S	47.00	90.00
1911	3.00	20.00
1911D	3.75	20.00
1911S	7.75	34.00

	F	XF
1912	2.75	20.00
1912D	3.75	20.00
1912S	5.50	29.00
1913	2.75	20.00
1913S	75.00	195.00
1914	3.00	20.00
1914D	3.50	20.00
1914S	7.25	5.00
1915	3.00	20.00
1915S	30.00	55.00
1916	3.25	20.00
1916S	4.75	20.00

MERCURY DIMES

The name Mercury for this dime is a misnomer. Designed by Adolph Weinman, it actually depicts Liberty wearing a winged cap, representing freedom of thought. It was received with wide acclaim for its artistic merit when it was first released as part of a program for the beautification of U.S. coinage. The reverse carries the ancient Roman fasces, a symbol of authority still seen in the U.S. Senate. The horizontal bands tying the fasces together do not always strike up distinctly from each other, and those coins with "full split bands" often command a premium.

Known Counterfeits: These include 1916D, 1921, 1921D, 1931D, 1942/1, 1942/1D, most of which have been made by altering the mint mark on a more common date. The date 1923D is a fantasy, none having been struck.

	VF	MS-60
1916	6.00	30.00
1916D	2,650.00	6,300.00
1916S	8.00	35.00
1917	4.75	28.00
1917D	21.00	120.00
1917S	5.50	62.00
1918	10.00	70.00
1918D	9.50	105.00
1918S	8.00	90.00
1919	5.00	37.00
1919D	20.00	175.00
1919S	13.00	175.00
1920	3.50	27.50
1920D	7.00	105.00

1916D Mercury Dime

	VF	MS-60
1920S	7.00	110.00
1921	260.00	1,000.00
1921D	335.00	1,100.00
1923	3.50	27.50
1923S	12.00	160.00
1924	4.25	42.00
1924D	13.00	160.00
1924S	8.75	170.00
1925	4.00	28.00
1925D	36.00	350.00
1925S	11.50	175.00
1926	2.75	25.00
1926D	8.00	110.00
1926S	45.00	870.00
1927	3.50	26.00
1927D	18.00	175.00
1927S	7.75	280.00
1928	3.50	27.50
1928D	17.00	170.00
1928S	5.50	110.00

1925D Mercury Dime

	VF	MS-60
1929	2.75	20.00
1929D	6.00	25.00
1929S	4.00	32.50
1930	3.50	26.00
1930S	5.50	70.00
1931	4.25	5.00
1931D	15.00	84.00
1931S	6.00	84.00
1934	3.00	20.00
1934D	4.00	45.00
1935	2.15	8.00
1935D	3.75	34.00
1935S	3.00	24.00
1936	2.25	8.00
1936D	3.00	26.00
1936S	2.50	20.00
1937	2.00	8.00
1937D	3.00	21.00
1937S	3.00	24.00
1938	2.25	13.00

1942 Mercury Dime

	VF	MS-60
1938D	3.50	16.00
1938S	2.35	20.00
1939	2.00	8.50
1939D	2.00	7.50
1939S	2.50	21.00
1940	1.10	6.00
1940D	1.10	7.00
1940S	1.10	7.00
1941	1.10	5.00
1941D	1.10	7.00
1941S	1.10	7.00
1942, 2 over 1	715.00	1,900.00
1942D, 2 over 1	680.00	1,900.00
1942	1.10	5.50
1942D	1.10	7.00
1942S	1.10	9.00
1943	1.10	5.50
1943D	1.10	7.50
1943S	1.10	8.25
1944	1.10	5.50

	VF	MS-60
1944D	1.10	6.00
1944S	1.10	6.50
1945	1.10	4.00
1945D	1.10	4.50
1945S	1.10	6.50
1945S micro S	3.00	23.00

ROOSEVELT DIMES

The fact that the dime was chosen to bear the image of Franklin Roosevelt is not a coincidence. It was selected to remind people of the President's involvement in the March of Dimes. He himself was crippled by polio. The coin was designed on a tight deadline by Chief Engraver John R. Sinnock. There are no true rarities in this series.

Known Counterfeits: Counterfeit Roosevelt dimes are quite rare.

	XF	BU
1946	.65	1.75
1946D	.65	1.75
1946S	.65	2.50
1947	.65	3.50

	XF	BU
1947D	.95	4.00
1947S	.95	3.00
1948	.95	3.00
1948D	1.20	2.50
1948S	.95	2.00
1949	1.50	15.00
1949D	1.25	4.50
1949S	2.75	18.00
1950	.95	3.00
1950D	.65	3.00
1950S	1.25	18.00
1950S, S over D	70.00	225.00
1951	.85	1.75
1951D	.65	1.75
1951S	1.05	7.00
1952	.90	1.65
1952D	.65	1.35
1952S	1.05	4.00
1953	.65	1.10
1953D	.65	1.00

	XF	BU
1953S	.65	1.00
1954	.65	1.00
1954D	.65	1.00
1954S	.65	1.00
1955	.80	1.00
1955D	.75	1.00
1955S	.65	1.00
1956	.60	1.00
1956D	.60	1.00
1957	.60	1.00
1957D	.60	1.00
1958	.60	1.00
1958D	.6	1.00
1959	.60	1.00
1959D	.60	1.00
1960	.60	1.00
1960D	.60	1.00
1961	.60	1.00
1961D	.60	1.00
1962	.60	1.00

1964 Roosevelt Dime

	XF	BU
1962D	.60	1.00
1963	.60	.95
1963D	.60	.95
1964	.60	.90
1964D	.60	.90

Cupro-Nickel Clad Copper	XF	BU
1965	—	.60
1966	—	.50
1967	—	.50
1968	—	.50
1968D	—	.50
1968S proof only	—	.75
1969	—	.50
1969D	—	.50
1969S proof only	—	.75
1970	—	.50
1970D	—	.50
1970S proof only	—	.75
1971	—	.50

1968 Roosevelt Dime with Cupro-Nickel Clad Copper

Cupro-Nickel Clad Copper	XF	BU
1971D	—	.50
1971S proof only	—	.75
1972	—	.50
1972D	—	.50
1972S proof only	—	1.00
1973	—	.50
1973D	—	.40
1973S proof only	—	1.00
1974	—	.40
1974D	—	.40
1974S proof only	—	1.25
1975	—	.50
1975D	—	.40
1975S proof only	—	1.50
1976	—	.50
1976D	—	.50
1976S proof only	—	1.00
1977	—	.40
1977D	—	.40

Cupro-Nickel Clad Copper	XF	BU
1977S proof only	—	1.75
1978	—	.40
1978D	—	.40
1978S proof only	—	1.25
1979	—	.40
1979D	—	.40
1979 thick S proof only	—	1.00
1979 thin S proof only	—	1.25
1980P	—	.40
1980D	—	.40
1980S proof only	—	1.00
1981P	—	.40
1981D	—	.40
1981S proof only	—	1.00
1982P	—	1.00
1982 no mint mark error	50.00	125.00
1982D	—	.50
1982S proof only	—	1.25
1983P	—	.50

Cupro-Nickel Clad Copper	XF	BU
1983D	—	.50
1983S proof only	—	1.25
1984P	—	.35
1984D	—	.50
1984S proof only	—	1.60
1985P	—	.50
1985D	—	.40
1985S proof only	—	1.10
1986P	—	.50
1986D	—	.35
1986S proof only	—	2.50
1987P	—	.35
1987D	—	.35
1987S proof only	—	1.25
1988P	—	.35
1988D	—	.35
1988S proof only	—	2.50
1989P	—	.35
1989D	—	.35

Cupro-Nickel Clad Copper	XF	BU
1989S proof only	—	**3.00**
1990P	—	**.35**
1990D	—	**.35**
1990S proof only	—	**2.75**
1991P	—	**.35**
1991D	—	**.35**
1991S proof only	—	**3.25**
1992P	—	**.35**
1992D	—	**.35**
1992S proof only	—	**3.40**
1992S Silver, proof only	—	**4.25**
1993P	—	**.35**
1993D	—	**.35**
1993S proof only	—	**5.85**
1993S Silver, proof only	—	**7.50**
1994P	—	**.35**
1994D	—	**.35**
1994S proof only	—	**5.00**
1994S Silver, proof only	—	**7.00**

Cupro-Nickel Clad Copper	XF	BU
1995	—	.35
1995D	—	.35
1995S proof only	—	5.00
1995S Silver, proof only	—	7.00
1996	—	.35
1996D	—	.35
1996W	—	12.00
1996S proof only	—	2.50
1996S Silver, proof only	—	7.50
1997P	—	.35
1997D	—	.35
1997S proof only	—	8.00
1997S Silver, proof only	—	20.00
1998P	—	.35
1998D	—	.35
1998S proof only	—	4.00
1998S Silver, proof only	—	8.00
1999P	—	.35
1999D	—	.35

Cupro-Nickel Clad Copper	XF	BU
1999S proof only	—	3.00
1999S Silver, proof only	—	5.00
2000P	—	.35
2000D	—	.35
2000S proof only	—	2.00
2000S Silver, proof only	—	5.00
2001P	—	.35
2001D	—	.35
2001S proof only	—	3.00
2001S Silver, proof only	—	5.50
2002P	—	.35
2002D	—	.35
2002S proof only	—	2.00
2002S Silver, proof only	—	5.00
2003P	—	.35
2003D	—	.35
2003S proof only	—	2.00
2003S Silver, proof only	—	5.00
2004P	—	.35

Cupro-Nickel Clad Copper	XF	BU
2004D	—	.35
2004S proof only	—	2.00
2004S Silver, proof only	—	5.00

TWENTY-CENT PIECES

It is evident that even before this coin's release, the mint was concerned about the public confusing it with a quarter. This is indicated by several features distinct from the other silver coins of the day. The reverse design is a mirror image of that on the others, the word LIBERTY on the shield is in relief rather than incuse, and the edge is plain, not reeded. Nevertheless, the public was still confused, and the coin was terminated after only two years in circulation, the 1877 and 1878 dates being collectors' issues.

Known Counterfeits: 1876CC with added mint mark. Some 19th century charlatans hand-scraped reeding into the edge of pieces in hopes of passing them off as quarters.

	VG	VF
1875	100.00	190.00
1875CC	120.00	225.00
1875S	90.00	130.00

	VG	VF
1876	150.00	300.00
1876CC Extremely Rare MS-65		148,500.00
1877	—	2,100.00
1878	—	1,800.00

1876 Twenty-Cent Piece

SEATED LIBERTY QUARTERS

Following the introduction of Christian Gobrecht's Seated Liberty design on the silver dollar, the smaller coins were gradually brought into harmony with this design. It is generally accepted that the seated goddess version of Liberty was directly or indirectly inspired by depictions of the Roman allegory of Britannia on British coins.

Several minor changes were implemented over the life of this coin. After the first few years, additional drapery was added below Liberty's elbow. The arrows by the date from 1853 to 1855, and the rays on the reverse in 1853 indicate a 7 percent reduction in weight, arrows in 1873 to 1874 a minuscule increase. A ribbon with the motto "In God We Trust" was added over the eagle in 1866.

Known Counterfeits: Genuine 1858 quarters have been re-engraved to pass as 1853 no arrows pieces. Contemporary counterfeits struck in copper, lead, and white metal (tin and lead alloys) exist.

No Motto Above Eagle	VG	VF
1838	27.00	65.00
1839	28.00	65.00
1840O	27.00	110.00

1847 Seated Liberty Quarter with No Motto Above Eagle

No Motto Above Eagle	VG	VF
1840 extra drapery from elbow	55.00	125.00
1840O extra drapery from elbow	50.00	120.00
1841	90.00	185.00
1841O	30.00	100.00
1842	120.00	275.00
1842O small date	650.00	1,850.00
1842O large date	27.00	45.00
1843	27.00	45.00
1843O	28.00	100.00
1844	27.00	45.00
1844O	27.00	60.00
1845	27.00	45.00
1846	27.00	50.00
1847	27.00	45.00
1847O	40.00	120.00
1848	55.00	185.00
1849	27.00	65.00
1849O	600.00	1,700.00
1850	45.00	110.00

No Motto Above Eagle	VG	VF
1850O	30.00	100.00
1851	75.00	225.00
1851O	265.00	575.00
1852	60.00	185.00
1852O	250.00	595.00
1853 no arrows	475.00	900.00

Arrows At Date	VG	VF
1853	27.00	45.00
1853, 3 over 4	65.50	200.00
1853O	35.00	100.00
1854	27.00	45.00
1854O	27.00	60.00
1854O huge O	150.00	285.00
1855	27.00	45.00
1855O	60.00	240.00
1855S	60.00	225.00

1853O Seated Liberty Quarter with
Arrrows at Date and Rays on Reverse

1856 Seated Liberty Quarter
with Arrows Removed From Date

Arrows Removed From Date	VG	VF
1856	27.00	45.00
1856O	30.00	60.00
1856S	65.00	250.00
1856S, S over S	100.00	375.00
1857	27.00	45.00
1857O	27.00	45.00
1857S	145.00	400.00
1858	27.00	45.00
1858O	30.00	70.00
1858S	100.00	275.00
1859	27.00	45.00
1859O	30.00	80.00
1859S	135.00	450.00
1860	27.00	45.00
1860O	30.00	55.00
1860S	325.00	900.00
1861	27.00	45.00
1861S	125.00	400.00
1862	27.00	45.00

Arrows Removed From Date	VG	VF
1862S	125.00	300.00
1863	45.00	120.00
1864	100.00	200.00
1864S	500.00	1,250.00
1865	100.00	200.00
1865S	135.00	350.00
Motto Above Eagle	VG	VF
1866	575.00	950.00
1866S	325.00	900.00
1867	300.00	625.00
1867S	350.00	900.00
1868	225.00	400.00
1868S	100.00	300.00
1869	425.00	675.00
1869S	125.00	375.00
1870	80.00	200.00
1870CC	5,000.00	12,000.00
1871	60.00	125.00

1873 Seated Liberty Quarter, Open 3, with Motto Above Eagle

Motto Above Eagle	VG	VF
1871CC	3,800.00	9,500.00
1871S	400.00	800.00
1872	40.00	110.00
1872CC	850.00	2,950.00
1872S	1,250.00	2,000.00
1873 closed 3	225.00	525.00
1873 open 3	42.50	120.00
1873CC four known		

Arrows At Date	VG	VF
1873	27.00	60.00
1873CC	3,500.00	8,500.00
1873S	40.00	140.00
1874	27.00	70.00
1874S	30.00	110.00

Arrows Removed From Date	VG	VF
1875	27.00	45.00
1875CC	90.00	300.00
1875S	36.00	110.00

1874S Seated Liberty Quarter with Arrows at Date

1879 Seated Liberty Quarter
with Arrows Removed From Date

Arrows Removed From Date	VG	VF
1876	27.00	45.00
1876CC	27.00	45.00
1876S	27.00	45.00
1877	27.00	45.00
1877CC	28.00	45.00
1877S	27.00	45.00
1877S over horizontal S	48.00	125.00
1878	27.00	45.00
1878CC	29.00	85.00
1878S	185.00	350.00
1879	235.00	325.00
1880	235.00	325.00
1881	250.00	350.00
1882	250.00	350.00
1883	265.00	365.00
1884	400.00	600.00
1885	265.00	365.00
1886	650.00	800.00
1887	350.00	485.00

Arrows Removed From Date	VG	VF
1888	300.00	420.00
1888S	27.00	45.00
1889	285.00	385.00
1890	85.00	125.00
1891	27.00	45.00
1891O	225.00	550.00
1891S	27.00	65.00

BARBER QUARTERS

The quarter, dime, and half dollar introduced in 1892 bear a portrait head of Liberty instead of an entire figure. They were designed by Chief Engraver Charles E. Barber, after whom they have been popularly named. More practical than artistically adventurous, contemporaries thought the design rather boring if not unpleasant. The reverse of the quarter and the half have a fully spread heraldic eagle, a ribbon in its beak, with a field of stars above. Barber quarters are very common, and well worn examples are often regarded as little better than bullion.

Known Counterfeits: 1913S suspected but not confirmed. Contemporary counterfeits in a tin-lead alloy are not rare.

1892 Barber Quarter

	F	XF
1892	22.00	70.00
1892O	35.00	82.00
1892S	75.00	150.00
1893	25.00	67.00
1893O	27.00	82.00
1893S	50.00	130.00
1894	30.00	90.00
1894O	36.00	90.00
1894S	36.00	90.00
1895	30.00	75.00
1895O	40.00	110.00
1895S	45.00	110.00
1896	25.00	77.00
1896O	90.00	375.00
1896S	1,250.00	2,950.00
1897	21.00	71.00
1897O	80.00	375.00
1897S	220.00	400.00
1898	22.00	71.00

	F	XF
1898O	65.00	235.00
1898S	42.00	75.00
1899	22.00	70.00
1899O	30.00	96.00
1899S	70.00	125.00
1900	21.00	70.00
1900O	62.00	125.00
1900S	38.00	75.00
1901	228.00	72.00
1901O	110.00	365.00
1901S	10,500.00	16,000.00
1902	17.00	65.00
1902O	45.00	120.00
1902S	47.00	130.00
1903	17.00	65.00
1903O	38.00	96.00
1903S	45.00	110.00
1904	17.50	65.00
1904O	50.00	190.00

1903 Barber Quarter

	F	XF
1905	26.00	72.00
1905O	80.00	225.00
1905S	40.00	100.00
1906	17.00	70.00
1906D	25.00	70.00
1906O	38.00	96.00
1907	17.00	65.00
1907D	27.00	80.00
1907O	17.00	70.00
1907S	42.00	115.00
1908	18.00	70.00
1908D	17.00	70.00
1908O	17.00	75.00
1908S	75.00	280.00
1909	17.00	65.00
1909D	20.00	75.00
1909O	85.00	315.00
1909S	30.00	70.00

	F	XF
1910	25.00	70.00
1910D	40.00	110.00
1911	17.00	72.00
1911D	87.00	300.00
1911S	50.00	150.00
1912	17.00	70.00
1912S	42.00	110.00
1913	70.00	400.00
1913D	34.00	80.00
1913S	2,850.00	5,300.00
1914	17.00	58.00
1914D	17.00	58.00
1914S	165.00	440.00
1915	17.00	65.00
1915D	17.00	65.00
1915S	27.00	80.00
1916	17.00	58.00
1916D	17.00	58.00

STANDING LIBERTY QUARTERS

According to many at the time, Hermon MacNeil's Standing Liberty quarter was America's first obscene coin. Many prominent artists, however, thought it an excellent example of inspired neo-classical art. In either case, it was very well debated at the time. Its original version, with a bare breasted Liberty stepping through a gateway while exposing a shield, was ultimately replaced by a more modest one on which she is clad in chain mail. The corrective legislation, however, was careful not to criticize the coin's artistic merit or moral standing openly, thus not offending the Commission of Fine Arts, responsible for its approval.

Technically, the coin shared with the Buffalo nickel the problem of a high relief date that wore off. This was partially remedied in 1925 by carving out the area of the date and placing it in the recess. Another technical problem with this quarter was the tendency of Liberty's head to be incompletely struck. As a result, high-grade pieces with fully struck heads command extra premiums. Examples with the date worn off are worth only their bullion value.

Known Counterfeits: 1916 altered from 1917, 1917 Type I, 1918S 8 over 7, 1923S (altered, including all with round topped 3), 1927S (altered).

1916 Standing Liberty Quarter

	F	XF
1916	6,750.00	9,500.00
1917	48.00	80.00
1917D	48.00	100.00
1917S	48.00	145.00
1917	27.00	48.00
1917D	65.00	94.00
1917S	62.00	77.00
1918	27.00	45.00
1918D	45.00	87.00
1918S	32.00	50.00
1918S, 8 over 7	2,500.00	5,900.00
1919	52.00	70.00
1919D	165.00	400.00
1919S	160.00	470.00
1920	24.00	40.00
1920D	75.00	125.00
1920S	28.00	55.00
1921	290.00	480.00
1923	28.00	40.00

	F	XF
1923S	450.00	750.00
1924	20.00	35.00
1924D	95.00	160.00
1924S	38.00	90.00
1925	5.00	34.00
1926	5.00	33.00
1926D	15.00	56.00
1926S	12.00	100.00
1927	5.00	32.00
1927D	19.00	115.00
1927S	65.00	1,000.00
1928	5.00	29.00
1928D	8.00	38.00
1928S	6.00	32.00
1929	5.00	30.00
1929D	6.00	34.00
1929S	5.00	30.00
1930	5.00	30.00
1930S	6.50	30.00

1927S Standing Liberty Quarter

WASHINGTON QUARTERS

The Washington quarter was intended to be a one year commemorative for the 200th anniversary of Washington's birth, not a regular issue. Its release was delayed because of the Treasury's decision to change designers from Laura Gardin Fraser to John Flanagan. Both designs were based on Houdon's 1785 bust of Washington. Eventually, it was decided to replace the unpopular Standing Liberty quarter with the new commemorative, which enjoyed immense initial popularity.

Several dates in the 1930s are characterized by weak rims, making grading difficult. 1934 and 1935 do not have this problem. 1964 pieces were aggressively hoarded in uncirculated rolls, and as such are excessively common.

A special reverse was used in 1975 and 1976 (both with 1976 obverse) to commemorate the American Bicentennial. It depicts the bust of a Colonial drummer designed by Jack L. Ahr.

Known Counterfeits: 1932D and 1932S exist with false mint marks. Counterfeits of high-grade 1932 and 1934 pieces also exist.

1936D Washington Quarter

	VF	BU
1932	7.50	24.00
1932D	155.00	1,000.00
1932S	145.00	425.00
1934	3.50	25.00
1934D	10.00	220.00
1935	2.75	21.00
1935D	10.00	220.00
1935S	6.00	85.00
1936	2.75	21.00
1936D	15.00	425.00
1936S	5.50	100.00
1937	3.55	22.00
1937D	5.00	60.00
1937S	11.50	120.00
1938	6.00	70.00
1938S	7.00	70.00
1939	2.50	20.00
1939D	4.50	37.00
1939S	6.50	75.00

1945 Washington Quarter

	VF	BU
1940	2.50	20.00
1940D	10.00	90.00
1940S	6.00	24.00
1941	2.00	10.00
1941D	3.00	30.00
1941S	2.50	30.00
1942	2.00	7.00
1942D	2.50	17.00
1942S	3.00	75.00
1943	2.00	5.00
1943D	3.50	26.00
1943S	5.00	30.00
1944	2.00	5.00
1944D	2.50	15.00
1944S	2.75	15.00
1945	1.75	5.00
1945D	3.00	17.00
1945S	2.50	10.00
1946	1.85	5.00

1953D Washington Quarter

	VF	BU
1946D	2.00	5.00
1946S	2.00	4.00
1947	2.25	6.00
1947D	2.25	4.50
1947S	2.25	4.00
1948	2.00	4.00
1948D	2.00	9.00
1948S	2.00	6.00
1949	3.00	30.00
1949D	2.50	20.00
1950	1.75	6.00
1950D	2.00	5.00
1950D, D over S	60.00	275.00
1950S	2.00	9.00
1950S, S over D	65.00	400.00
1951	1.75	6.00
1951D	2.00	6.00
1951S	3.75	17.00
1952	1.75	6.00

	VF	BU
1952D	1.75	5.00
1952S	1.75	15.00
1953	1.75	5.00
1953D	1.75	4.00
1953S	1.75	5.00
1954	1.50	4.00
1954D	1.50	5.00
1954S	1.50	3.75
1955	1.65	3.50
1955D	2.00	4.00
1956	1.65	4.00
1956D	1.75	3.00
1957	—	3.50
1957D	—	2.50
1958	—	2.75
1958D	—	2.50
1959	—	2.75
1959D	—	2.75
1960	—	2.25

	VF	BU
1960D	—	2.25
1961	—	2.25
1961D	—	2.25
1962	—	2.25
1962D	—	2.25
1963	—	2.00
1963D	—	2.00
1964	—	2.00
1964D	—	2.00

Cupro-Nickel Clad Copper	VF	BU
1965	—	1.00
1966	—	1.00
1967	—	1.00
1968	—	1.00
1968D	—	1.25
1968S proof only	—	2.50
1969	—	1.25
1969D	—	1.00

1966 Washington Quarter with Cupro-Nickel Clad Copper

Cupro-Nickel Clad Copper	VF	BU
1969S proof only	—	2.50
1970	—	1.00
1970D	—	1.00
1970S proof only	—	2.00
1971	—	1.00
1971D	—	1.00
1971S proof only	—	2.00
1972	—	.75
1972D	—	.75
1972S proof only	—	2.00
1973	—	.75
1973D	—	1.00
1973S proof only	—	2.00
1974	—	.75
1974D	—	1.00
1974S proof only	—	2.00
1976 bicentennial	—	1.00
1976D bicentennial	—	1.00
1976S bicentennial, proof only	—	2.00

Cupro-Nickel Clad Copper	VF	BU
1976S bicentennial, Silver Clad	—	3.00
1977	—	.75
1977D	—	.75
1977S proof only	—	2.00
1978	—	.75
1978D	—	.75
1978S proof only	—	2.00
1979	—	.75
1979D	—	.75
1979 thick S, proof only	—	2.00
1979 thin S, proof only	—	3.00
1980P	—	.75
1980D	—	.75
1980S proof only	—	2.00
1981P	—	.75
1981D	—	.75
1981S proof only	—	2.00
1982P	—	3.00
1982D	—	1.50

Cupro-Nickel Clad Copper	VF	BU
1982S proof only	—	3.00
1983P	—	3.00
1983D	—	2.00
1983S proof only	—	2.75
1984P	—	1.00
1984D	—	1.25
1984S proof only	—	2.75
1985P	—	1.50
1985D	—	2.00
1985S proof only	—	1.75
1986P	—	3.00
1986D	—	2.00
1986S proof only	—	3.00
1987P	—	.75
1987D	—	.75
1987S proof only	—	2.00
1988P	—	1.00
1988D	—	1.00
1988S proof only	—	2.25

Cupro-Nickel Clad Copper	VF	BU
1989P	—	.75
1989D	—	.75
1989S proof only	—	**2.25**
1990P	—	.75
1990D	—	.75
1990S proof only	—	**6.00**
1991P	—	.75
1991D	—	.75
1991S proof only	—	**3.00**
1992P	—	.75
1992D	—	.75
1992S proof only	—	**3.25**
1992S Silver, proof only	—	**4.00**
1993P	—	.75
1993D	—	.75
1993S proof only	—	**3.00**
1993S Silver, proofonly	—	**8.55**
1994P	—	.75
1994D	—	.75

Cupro-Nickel Clad Copper	VF	BU
1994S proof only	—	4.00
1994S Silver, proof only	—	12.50
1995P	—	.75
1995D	—	.75
1995S proof only	—	18.00
1995S Silver, proof only	—	18.00
1996P	—	.75
1996D	—	.75
1996S proof only	—	4.50
1996S Silver, proof only	—	11.50
1997P	—	.75
1997D	—	.75
1997S proof only	—	10.00
1997S Silver, proof only	—	20.00
1998P	—	.75
1998D	—	.75
1998S proof only	—	11.00
1998S Silver, proof only	—	10.50

STATE QUARTERS

In 1992, to commemorate its 125th anniversary, Canada released a set of circulating commemorative quarters honoring each province and territory. They became immensely popular with the general public. Partially inspired by this Canadian series, the United States has begun issuing a similar set of quarters honoring the 50 states. It was the intent of Congress to "promote the diffusion of knowledge among the youth of the United States about the individual states, their history and geography, and the rich diversity of the national heritage."

Five will be released each year from 1999 to 2008. Their release dates will be in the order by which each state ratified the Constitution, with a new quarter appearing roughly every 10 weeks. These will be the only quarters issued during these years. None with the eagle reverse will be produced at all.

The designs must meet certain federal criteria, but will be designed and submitted at state level. Many will be provided by public competitions.

In addition to clad circulation strikes, special silver and clad proof coins will be produced for collectors, much as they have been in previous years.

Known Counterfeits: Apparently risqué designs are actually satirical tokens struck with privately made dies on real quarters.

State Quarter Front

Delaware (1999)

Pennsylvania (1999)

New Jersey (1999)

Georgia (1999)

Connecticut (1999)

Massachusetts (2000)

Maryland (2000)

South Carolina (2000)

New Hampshire (2000)

Virginia (2000)

New York (2001)

	BU	PF
1999P Delaware	1.50	—
1999D Delaware	1.50	—
1999S Delaware proof only	—	20.00
1999S Delaware Silver, proof only	—	40.00
1999P Pennsylvania	1.50	—
1999D Pennsylvania	1.50	—
1999S Pennsylvania proof only	—	15.00
1999S Pennsylvania Silver, proof only	—	40.50
1999P New Jersey	1.50	—
1999D New Jersey	1.50	—
1999S New Jersey proof only	—	15.00
1999S New Jersey Silver, proof only	—	40.00
1999P Georgia	.75	—
1999D Georgia	.75	—
1999S Georgia proof only	—	15.00
1999S Georgia Silver, proof only	—	40.00
1999P Connecticut	.75	—
1999D Connecticut	.75	—

North Carolina (2001)

Rhode Island (2001)

Vermont (2001)

Kentucky (2001)

	BU	PF
1999S Connecticut proof only	—	15.00
1999S Connecticut Silver, proof only	—	40.00
2000P Massachusetts	.75	—
2000D Massachusetts	.75	—
2000S Massachusetts proof only	—	5.00
2000S Massachusetts Silver, proof only	—	10.00
2000P Maryland	.75	—
2000D Maryland	.75	—
2000S Maryland proof only	—	5.00
2000S Maryland Silver, proof only	—	10.00
2000P South Carolina	.75	—
2000D South Carolina	.75	—
2000S South Carolina proof only	—	5.00
2000S South Carolina Silver, proof only	—	10.00
2000P New Hampshire	.75	—
2000D New Hampshire	.75	—

	BU	PF
2000S New Hampshire, proof only	—	5.00
2000S New Hampshire Silver, proof only	—	10.00
2000P Virginia	.75	—
2000D Virginia	.75	—
2000S Virginia, proof only	—	5.00
2000S Virginia Silver, proof only	—	10.00
2001P New York	.75	—
2001D NewYork	.75	—
2001S New York proof only	—	7.50
2001S New York Silver, proof only	—	22.50
2001P North Carolina	.75	—
2001D North Carolina	.75	—
2001S North Carolina proof only	—	7.50
2001S North Carolina Silver, proof only	—	22.50
2001P Rhode Island	.75	—
2001D Rhode Island	.75	—
2001S Rhode Island proof only	—	7.50

Tennesee (2002)

Ohio (2002)

Louisiana (2002)

Indiana (2002)

Mississippi (2002)

Illinois (2003)

Alabama (2003)

Maine (2003)

Missouri (2003)

Arkansas (2003)

Michigan (2004)

Florida (2004)

Texas (2004)

Iowa (2004)

Wisconsin (2004)

California (2005)

	BU	PF
2001S Rhode Island Silver, proof only	—	22.50
2001P Vermont	1.00	—
2001D Vermont	.75	—
2001S Vermont proof only	—	7.50
2001S Vermont Silver, proof only	—	22.50
2001P Kentucky	1.00	—
2001D Kentucky	.75	—
2001S Kentucky proof only	—	7.50
2001S Kentucky Silver, proof only	—	22.50
2002P Tennessee	1.00	—
2002D Tennessee	1.00	—
2002S Tennessee proof only	—	6.00
2002S Tennessee Silver, proof only	—	18.00
2002P Ohio	.75	—
2002D Ohio	.75	—
2002S Ohio proof only	—	6.00
2002S Ohio Silver, proof only	—	18.00
2002P Louisiana	.75	—

Minnesota (2005)

Oregon (2005)

Kansas (2005)

West Virginia (2005)

	BU	PF
2002D Louisiana	.75	—
2002S Louisiana proof only	—	6.00
2002S Louisiana Silver, proof only	—	18.00
2002P Indiana	.75	—
2002D Indiana	.75	—
2002S Indiana proof only	—	6.00
2002S Indiana Silver, proof only	—	18.00
2002P Mississippi	.75	—
2002D Mississippi	.75	—
2002S Mississippi proof only	—	6.00
2002S Mississippi Silver, proof only	—	18.00
2003P Illinois	.75	—
2003D Illinois	.75	—
2003S Illinois proof only	—	6.00
2003S Illinois Silver, proof only	—	10.00
2003P Alabama	.75	—
2003D Alabama	.75	—
2003S Alabama proof only	—	6.00
2003S Alabama Silver, proof only	—	10.00

	BU	PF
2003P Maine	.75	—
2003D Maine	.75	—
2003S Maine proof only	—	6.00
2003S Maine Silver, proof only	—	10.00
2003P Missouri	.75	—
2003D Missouri	.75	—
2003S Missouri proof only	—	6.00
2003S Missouri Silver, proof only	—	10.00
2003P Arkansas	.75	—
2003D Arkansas	.75	—
2003S Arkansas proof only	—	6.00
2003S Arkansas Silver, proof only	—	10.00
2004P Michigan	.75	—
2004D Michigan	.75	—
2004S Michigan proof only	—	6.00
2004S Michigan Silver, proof only	—	10.00
2004P Florida	.75	—
2004D Florida	.75	—
2004S Florida proof only	—	6.00

	BU	PF
2004S Florida Silver, proof only	—	10.00
2004P Texas	.75	—
2004D Texas	.75	—
2004S Texas proof only	—	6.00
2004S Texas Silver, proof only	—	15.00
2004P Iowa	.75	—
2004D Iowa	.75	—
2004S Iowa proof only	—	6.00
2004S Iowa Silver, proof only	—	10.00
2004P Wisconsin	.75	—
2004D Wisconsin (3 varieties)	.75	—
2004S Wisconsin proof only	—	6.00
2004S Wisconsin Silver, proof only	—	10.00
2005P California	.75	—
2005D California	.75	—
2005S California proof only	—	5.00
2005S California Silver, proof only	—	8.00
2005P Minnesota	.75	—
2005D Minnesota	.75	—

	BU	PF
2005S Minnesota proof only	—	**5.00**
2005S Minnesota Silver, proof only	—	**8.00**
2005P Oregon	.75	
2005D Oregon	.75	
2005S Oregon proof only	—	**5.00**
2005S Oregon Silver, proof only	—	**8.00**
2005P Kansas	.75	
2005D Kansas	.75	
2005S Kansas proof only	—	**5.00**
2005S Kansas Silver proof only	—	**8.00**
2005P West Virginia	.75	
2005D West Virginia	.75	
2005S West Virginia proof only	—	**5.00**
2005S West Virginia Silver, proof only	—	**8.00**

SEATED LIBERTY HALF DOLLARS

Following the introduction of Christian Gobrecht's Seated Liberty design on the silver dollar, smaller coins were gradually brought into harmony with this design. The half dollar was the last to make the change. It is generally accepted that the seated goddess version of Liberty was directly or indirectly inspired by depictions of the Roman allegory of Britannia on British coins. Several minor changes were adopted over the life of this coin. During its first year, additional drapery was added below Liberty's elbow. The arrows by the date from 1853 to 1855, and the rays on the reverse in 1853 indicate a 7-percent reduction in weight, arrows in 1873 to 1874 a minuscule increase. Most of the 1861O pieces were struck after Louisiana seceded from the Union. A ribbon with the motto "In God We Trust" was added over the eagle in 1866. Seated halves are often found cleaned. Be careful of retoned specimens.

Known Counterfeits: Genuine 1858O halves have been re-engraved to pass as 1853O no-arrows pieces. Some with-arrows pieces have had the arrows removed for the same reason. Contemporary counterfeits struck in tin and lead alloys are often found.

No Motto Above Eagle	VG	VF
1839 no drapery below elbow	65.00	315.00
1839 with drapery	35.00	75.00
1840 sm. rev. letters	35.00	70.00
1840 med. rev. letters (struck at New Orleans with 1838 reverse die)	175.00	325.00
1840O	35.00	80.00
1841	50.00	130.00
1841O	35.00	85.00
1842 small date	42.00	110.00
1842 large date	35.00	70.00
1842O small date	850.00	2,250.00
1842O large date	35.00	115.00
1843	35.00	70.00
1843O	35.00	70.00
1844	35.00	70.00
1844O	35.00	70.00
1844O double date	775.00	1,375.00
1845	40.00	110.00
1845O	35.00	70.00

No Motto Above Eagle	VG	VF
1845O no drapery	35.00	115.00
1846	35.00	70.00
1846, 6 over horizontal 6	235.00	400.00
1846O, med. date	35.00	70.00
1846O, tall date	245.00	575.00
1847, 7 over 6	2,750.00	4,250.00
1847	35.00	70.00
1847O	35.00	70.00
1848	60.00	170.00
1848O	35.00	70.00
1849	40.00	90.00
1849O	35.00	70.00
1850	300.00	500.00
1850O	35.00	80.00
1851	400.00	900.00
1851O	45.00	105.00
1852	500.00	850.00
1852O	125.00	350.00
1853O no arrows	154,000.00	rare

1839 Seated Liberty Half Dollar with
No Motto Above Eagle and No Drapery Below Elbow

Arrows At Date/ Rays On Reverse	VG	VF
1853	35.00	90.00
1853O	35.00	125.00

Arrows At Date/No Rays	VG	VF
1854	35.00	70.00
1854O	35.00	70.00
1855 over 1854	60.00	125.00
1855	35.00	75.00
1855O	35.00	70.00
1855S	350.00	1,300.00

Arrows Removed From Date	VG	VF
1856	35.00	70.00
1856O	35.00	70.00
1856S	80.00	260.00
1857	35.00	70.00
1857O	35.00	70.00
1857S	115.00	285.00
1858	35.00	70.00
1858O	35.00	70.00

*1853 Seated Liberty Half Dollar
with Arrows at Date and Rays on Reverse*

*1854 Seated Liberty Half Dollar
with Arrows at Date, No Rays on Reverse*

SEATED LIBERTY HALF DOLLARS

Arrows Removed From Date	VG	VF
1858S	35.00	95.00
1859	35.00	70.00
1859O	35.00	70.00
1859S	38.00	85.00
1860	35.00	80.00
1860O	35.00	70.00
1860S	35.00	75.00
1861	35.00	70.00
1861O	35.00	70.00
1861S	35.00	70.00
1862	40.00	95.00
1862S	35.00	70.00
1863	35.00	75.00
1863S	35.00	70.00
1864	35.00	95.00
1864S	35.00	70.00
1865	37.00	85.00
1865S	35.00	70.00
1866	—	unique
1866S	125.00	375.00

*1858S Seated Liberty Half Dollar
with Arrows Removed From Date*

Motto Above Eagle	VG	VF
1866	35.00	70.00
1866S	35.00	70.00
1867	35.00	90.00
1867S	35.00	70.00
1868	49.00	135.00
1868S	35.00	70.00
1869	35.00	70.00
1869S	35.00	70.00
1870	35.00	70.00
1870CC	1,200.00	3,000.00
1870S	35.00	70.00
1871	35.00	70.00
1871CC	325.00	1,200.00
1871S	35.00	70.00
1872	35.00	70.00
1872CC	100.00	325.00
1872S	33.00	110.00
1873 closed 3	35.00	90.00
1873 open 3	2,700.00	5,500.00

1872CC Seated Liberty Half Dollar with Motto Above Eagle

Motto Above Eagle	VG	VF
1873CC	220.00	800.00
1873S	no known specimens	

Arrows At Date	VG	VF
1873	35.00	85.00
1873CC	220.00	725.00
1873S	70.00	225.00
1874	35.00	85.00
1874CC	550.00	1,500.00
1874S	40.00	160.00

Arrows Removed From Date	VG	VF
1875	35.00	70.00
1875CC	35.00	95.00
1875S	35.00	70.00
1876	35.00	70.00
1876CC	35.00	85.00
1876S	35.00	70.00
1877	35.00	70.00

1873 Seated Liberty Half Dollar with Arrows at Date

Arrows Removed From Date	VG	VF
1877CC	33.00	75.00
1877S	35.00	70.00
1878	35.00	70.00
1878CC	525.00	1,250.00
1878S	17,500.00	27,500.00
1879	325.00	425.00
1880	310.00	410.00
1881	300.00	400.00
1882	400.00	500.00
1883	320.00	420.00
1884	425.00	550.00
1885	400.00	500.00
1886	425.00	575.00
1887	500.00	750.00
1888	315.00	400.00
1889	310.00	410.00
1890	310.00	410.00
1891	60.00	120.00

1878S Seated Liberty Half Dollar
with Arrows Removed From Date

BARBER HALF DOLLARS

The half dollar, quarter, and dime introduced in 1892 bear a portrait of Liberty's head, instead of an entire figure. They were designed by Chief Engraver Charles E. Barber, after whom they have been popularly named. Rather practical than artistically adventurous, contemporaries thought the design rather boring, if not unpleasant. The reverse of the half and the quarter have a fully spread heraldic eagle, a ribbon in its beak, with a field of stars above. This new design for the half dollar came only a year following its resurrection as an actively minted denomination.

Barbers are very common, and well-worn examples are often regarded as little better than bullion. Strong middle grades, on the other hand, are surprisingly difficult to obtain.

Known Counterfeits: Contemporary counterfeits in a tin-lead alloy are not rare. Altered 1913, 1914, and 1915 coins exist with mint marks removed.

	VG	VF
1892	38.00	115.00
1892O	300.00	485.00
1892S	300.00	395.00
1893	25.00	110.00
1893O	55.00	165.00
1893S	165.00	410.00

1892 Barber Half Dollar

	VG	VF
1894	40.00	130.00
1894O	28.00	125.00
1894S	22.00	100.00
1895	19.00	110.00
1895O	30.00	140.00
1895S	46.00	180.00
1896	23.00	130.00
1896O	40.00	225.00
1896S	120.00	280.00
1897	12.00	85.00
1897O	170.00	750.00
1897S	195.00	475.00
1898	13.00	85.00
1898O	60.00	300.00
1898S	39.00	116.00
1899	12.00	85.00
1899O	23.00	120.00
1899S	28.00	110.00
1900	14.00	85.00

	VG	VF
1900O	19.00	120.00
1900S	13.00	95.00
1901	12.00	75.00
1901O	20.00	145.00
1901S	39.00	300.00
1902	12.00	75.00
1902O	14.00	95.00
1902S	18.00	115.00
1903	13.00	95.00
1903O	13.00	95.00
1903S	13.00	95.00
1904	12.00	80.00
1904O	23.00	150.00
1904S	52.00	480.00
1905	23.00	130.00
1905O	37.00	200.00
1905S	13.00	100.00
1906	11.00	80.00
1906D	11.00	85.00

1903 Barber Half Dollar

	VG	VF
1906O	11.00	90.00
1906S	14.00	100.00
1907	11.00	80.00
1907D	11.00	80.00
1907O	11.00	85.00
1907S	18.00	135.00
1908	11.00	80.00
1908D	11.00	80.00
1908O	11.00	80.00
1908S	12.00	100.00
1909	15.00	60.00
1909O	15.00	114.00
1909S	11.00	91.00
1910	20.00	150.00
1910S	13.00	90.00
1911	11.00	70.00
1911D	13.00	85.00
1911S	11.00	84.00
1912	11.00	70.00

1908O Barber Half Dollar

	VG	VF
1912D	11.00	70.00
1912S	11.00	81.00
1913	45.00	275.00
1913D	13.00	83.00
1913S	11.00	90.00
1914	65.00	395.00
1914S	14.00	81.00
1915	52.00	270.00
1915D	11.00	77.00
1915S	12.00	75.00

WALKING LIBERTY HALF DOLLARS

This artistic new half dollar was designed by Adolph Weinman, the designer of the Mercury dime released in the same year. It depicts Liberty, the American flag draped about her and flowing in the breeze, progressing towards the dawn of a new day. It was received with wide acclaim for its artistic merit when it was first released as part of a program for the beautification of United States coinage. The reverse carries an eagle perched on a rocky crag. The obverse design proved so popular that it was resurrected in 1986 for use on the new silver one-ounce bullion coins.

Originally, the mint marks on this coin appeared on the obverse, but after a matter of months they were moved to the reverse.

Due to the arrangement of the design, Liberty's head does not always strike up fully. High-grade examples with fully struck heads are worth more.

Known Counterfeits: 1916S, 1938D coins with added mint mark exist. 1928D halves are all counterfeit.

	F	XF
1916	70.00	185.00
1916D	60.00	180.00
1916S	220.00	580.00
1917	9.00	40.00
1917D obv.	60.00	190.00
1917D rev.	34.00	255.00
1917S obv.	90.00	700.00
1917S rev.	16.00	50.00
1918	16.00	150.00
1918D	27.00	185.00
1918S	15.00	62.00
1919	60.00	450.00
1919D	67.50	650.00

	F	XF
1919S	43.00	790.00
1920	16.00	70.00
1920D	47.50	420.00
1920S	17.00	235.00
1921	275.00	1,500.00
1921D	400.00	2,100.00
1921S	190.00	4,800.00
1923S	24.00	250.00
1927S	13.00	125.00
1928S	14.00	150.00
1929D	13.00	90.00
1929S	12.00	90.00
1933S	12.00	52.00
1934	3.75	9.00
1934D	6.00	29.00
1934S	4.25	27.00
1935	3.75	6.75
1935D	6.00	29.50

1921D Walking Liberty Half Dollar

	F	XF
1935S	3.75	27.00
1936	3.75	6.00
1936D	4.00	20.00
1936S	4.00	21.00
1937	3.75	8.00
1937D	6.00	29.00
1937S	5.00	23.00
1938	6.00	10.00
1938D	75.00	100.00
1939	3.75	6.00
1939D	3.75	7.50
1939S	6.00	19.00
1940	4.00	6.00
1940S	4.00	8.00
1941	4.00	8.00
1941D	4.00	6.00
1941S	4.00	6.00
1942	4.00	5.00
1942D	4.00	6.00

	F	XF
1942D, D over S	42.00	80.00
1942S	4.00	6.00
1943	4.00	5.00
1943D	4.00	6.00
1943S	4.00	6.00
1944	4.00	5.00
1944D	4.00	6.00
1944S	4.00	6.25
1945	4.00	5.50
1945D	4.00	6.00
1945S	4.00	6.00
1946	4.00	5.50
1946D	6.25	15.00
1946S	4.00	6.25
1947	4.00	9.00
1947D	4.00	10.00

1944 Walking Liberty Half Dollar

FRANKLIN HALF DOLLARS

Like the design for the Washington Quarter, the design for the Franklin Half Dollar was used in opposition to the recommendation of the Commission of Fine Arts. The reverse depicts the Liberty Bell as its prime motif, despite a law requiring all coins larger than a dime to bear an eagle. This is why a small eagle was added at the side of the bell as an afterthought. While the coin was designed by Chief Engraver John R. Sinnock, the minute eagle was actually engraved by a young Frank Gasparro.

The most striking problem of the Franklin Half Dollar is the horizontal lines on the Liberty Bell. Mint-state examples with fully struck bell lines often sell for significantly more.

Known Counterfeits: It is possible that none exist.

	XF	MS-60
1948	6.50	13.75
1948D	5.50	10.00
1949	6.00	45.00
1949D	8.00	35.00
1949S	11.00	55.00
1950	6.00	26.00
1950D	7.50	22.00

	XF	MS-60
1951	4.50	10.00
1951D	8.00	21.00
1951S	4.00	18.00
1952	3.75	8.00
1952D	3.75	8.00
1952S	10.00	38.00
1953	6.00	16.00
1953D	4.00	7.00
1953S	6.00	24.00
1954	4.00	7.00
1954D	3.50	6.50
1954S	6.00	9.00
1955	19.00	30.00
1955 "Bugs Bunny" teeth	—	22.00
1956	5.00	7.00
1957	4.00	6.00
1957D	3.25	5.00
1958	3.50	5.00
1958D	3.00	4.75

1953 Franklin Half Dollar

1962 Franklin Half Dollar

	XF	MS-60
1959	2.90	4.50
1959D	2.90	5.00
1960	2.90	4.25
1960D	2.90	4.50
1961	2.90	4.25
1961D	2.90	4.50
1962	2.90	4.25
1962D	2.90	4.25
1963	2.90	4.00
1963D	2.90	4.00

KENNEDY HALF DOLLARS

Only three days had elapsed between the assassination of President John F. Kennedy on November 22, 1963, and the first notice from the director of the mint to the chief engraver to prepare for the issue of a coin bearing his portrait. Gilroy Roberts fashioned its obverse portrait based on the Kennedy inaugural medal to save time. The reverse is Frank Gasparro's rendition of the presidential seal. Remarkably, working dies were ready by January 2.

Kennedy halves have been struck in three different compositions. The 1964 issue was struck in the traditional 90-percent silver alloy. The following year, when dimes and quarters were changed to cupro-nickel clad copper, the half dollar was preserved as a silver alloy coin by striking it in a silver-clad version containing 80 percent silver in its outer layers, and 21 percent silver in its middle layer. The remaining alloy was copper. Finally, silver was abandoned in 1971, and only sporadic collectors issues have been struck in that metal since.

Circulation issues are now struck in the same clad composition as dimes and quarters. Coins dated 1970D, 1987P and 1987D were not issued to circulation, but are widely available from broken up mint sets.

A special reverse was used in 1975 and 1976 (both with 1976 obverse) to commemorate the American Bicentennial. It depicts Independence Hall in Philadelphia, designed by Seth G. Huntington.

Known Counterfeits: It is possible that none exist.

	BU
1964	**3.00**
1964D	**3.50**
Silver Clad	
1965	**1.35**
1966	**1.40**

Silver Clad	BU
1967	1.50
1968D	1.35
1968S proof only	5.00
1969D	1.35
1969S proof only	5.00
1970D	10.00
1970S proof only	9.50

Cupro-Nickel Clad Copper	BU
1971	1.55
1971D	1.00
1971S proof only	3.00
1972	1.25
1972D	1.25
1972S proof only	2.50
1973	1.25
1973D	1.25
1973S proof only	2.50

Cupro-Nickel Clad Copper	BU
1974	1.25
1974D	1.25
1974S proof only	3.00

Bicentennial Reverse	BU
1976 bicentennial	1.25
1976D bicentennial	1.00
1976S bicentennial proof only	1.75
1976S bicentennial Silver Clad	3.50

Regular Issue (Non Bicentennial) Continued	BU
1977	1.25
1977D	1.25
1977S proof only	3.00
1978	1.25
1978D	1.25
1978S proof only	2.50
1979	1.25
1979D	1.25

1976 Kennedy Half Dollar with Bicentennial on Reverse

Regular Issue (Non Bicentennial) Continued	BU
1979 filled S proof only	**2.50**
1979 clear S proof only	**18.00**
1980P	**1.25**
1980D	**1.25**
1980S proof only	**3.00**
1981P	**1.00**
1981D	**1.00**
1981S proof only	**3.00**
1982P	**1.25**
1982D	**1.25**
1982S proof only	**3.50**
1983P	**1.25**
1983D	**1.25**
1983S proof only	**3.50**
1984P	**1.25**
1984D	**1.25**
1984S proof only	**5.00**
1985P	**1.25**

Regular Issue (Non Bicentennial) Continued	BU
1985D	1.25
1985S proof only	4.50
1986P	4.00
1986D	3.00
1986S proof only	12.50
1987P	3.00
1987D	3.00
1987S proof only	4.00
1988P	1.25
1988D	1.25
1988S proof only	8.00
1989P	1.50
1989D	1.50
1989S proof only	8.00
1990P	2.00
1990D	2.00
1990S proof only	7.00
1991P	1.25

Regular Issue (Non Bicentennial) Continued	BU
1991D	1.25
1991S proof only	14.50
1992P	1.25
1992D	1.25
1992S proof only	10.00
1992S Silver, proof only	15.00
1993P	1.50
1993D	1.50
1993S proof only	14.00
1993S Silver, proof only	25.00
1994P	1.50
1994D	1.50
1994S proof only	11.00
1994S Silver, proof only	35.00
1995P	1.50
1995D	1.50
1995S proof only	47.50
1995S Silver, proof only	90.00

Regular Issue (Non Bicentennial) Continued	BU
1996P	2.00
1996D	2.00
1996S proof only	10.00
1996S Silver, proof only	50.00
1997P	2.00
1997D	2.00
1997S proof only	25.00
1997S Silver, proof only	100.00
1998P	2.00
1998D	2.00
1998S proof only	18.00
1998S Matte proof only	370.00
1998S Silver, proof only	30.00
1999P	2.00
1999D	2.00
1999S proof only	10.00
1999S Silver, proof only	25.00
2000P	2.00

Regular Issue (Non Bicentennial) Continued	BU
2000D	2.00
2000S proof only	7.00
2000S Silver, proof only	12.50
2001P	2.00
2001D	2.00
2001S proof only	7.00
2001S Silver, proof only	12.50
2002P	3.50
2002D	3.50
2002S proof only	15.00
2002S Silver, proof only	12.50
2003P	3.00
2003D	3.00
2003S proof only	8.00
2003S Silver, proof only	12.50
2004P	2.00
2004D	2.00
2004S proof only	8.00
2004S Silver, proof only	12.50

SEATED LIBERTY DOLLARS

The active production of silver dollars was finally resumed in 1840. However, the reverse design especially created for them was replaced by a more mundane heraldic eagle, similar to that in use on minor coinage. While production of these coins continued for most years, those struck from 1853 to about 1867 were primarily intended as bullion pieces for export, each containing more than a dollar's worth of silver. A ribbon with the motto " In God We Trust" was added over the eagle in 1866. These dollars are often found cleaned. Be careful of retoned specimens as well.

Known Counterfeits: Counterfeits of this type are not common.

No Motto Above Eagle	F	EF
1840	265.00	525.00
1841	265.00	425.00
1842	265.00	425.00
1843	265.00	370.00
1844	300.00	500.00
1845	285.00	550.00
1846	265.00	425.00
1846O	300.00	1,250.00
1847	265.00	425.00

1845 Seated Liberty Dollar with No Motto Above Eagle

No Motto Above Eagle	F	XF
1848	425.00	750.00
1849	265.00	425.00
1850	700.00	1,100.00
1850O	375.00	1,400.00
1851 original	8,000.00	13,500.00
1851 restrike proof	—	21,000.00
1852 original	6,500.00	11,500.00
1852 restrike proof	—	20,000.00
1853	285.00	600.00
1854	1,600.00	3,700.00
1855	1,400.00	3,650.00
1856	600.00	975.00
1857	550.00	1,100.00
1858	3,350.00	5,500.00
1859	265.00	600.00
1859O	265.00	425.00
1859S	400.00	1,350.00
1860	275.00	475.00
1860O	265.00	425.00

No Motto Above Eagle	F	XF
1861	650.00	1,250.00
1862	675.00	1,200.00
1863	450.00	990.00
1864	315.00	675.00
1865	290.00	625.00
1866	two known	

Motto Above Eagle	F	EF
1866	285.00	550.00
1867	300.00	600.00
1868	265.00	525.00
1869	265.00	440.00
1870	265.00	440.00
1870CC	500.00	1,450.00
1870S	60,000.00	175,000.00
1871	265.00	425.00
1871CC	3,750.00	8,950.00
1872	265.00	425.00
1872CC	1,750.00	4,250.00
1872S	400.00	1,100.00

1871 Seated Liberty Dollar with Motto Above Eagle

Motto Above Eagle	F	EF
1873	265.00	425.00
1873CC	6,500.00	17,500.00
1873S		none known to exist

TRADE DOLLARS

Trade dollars were coins struck deliberately for export as bullion, usually to the Far East. They were chiefly intended to compete against the Mexican peso, which had slightly more silver than a standard dollar. They were distinguished by a Liberty and eagle facing the opposite direction from the standard dollars.

From the very beginning, the legal tender status of Trade Dollars was limited in the United States, but in 1876 when the price of silver dropped, they ceased to have legal tender altogether, not having it restored until 1965! Eight million were redeemed by the government in 1887. Any struck between 1879 and 1885 are Proof Only collectors' issues. Prices listed for them are for circulated examples.

It was typical for Oriental merchants to impress a character into these and other silver coins to confirm that they accepted them as good quality. These "chop marks" are commonly found on trade dollars, sometimes in quantity. They reduce the value of the coin as they are considered a form of mutilation, but have recently been the subject of serious research. Chop-marked dollars may not be as valuable, but are still collectible.

Known Counterfeits: Counterfeits are not abundant and are more likely to be contemporary counterfeits. Be cautious of cleaned coins.

	F	EF
1873	125.00	250.00
1873CC	225.00	700.00
1873S	160.00	260.00
1874	150.00	240.00
1874CC	125.00	240.00
1874S	125.00	175.00
1875	400.00	650.00
1875CC	125.00	200.00
1875S	125.00	175.00
1875S, S over CC	400.00	695.00
1876	125.00	175.00
1876CC	200.00	375.00
1876S	125.00	175.00
1877	125.00	175.00

1876 Trade Dollar

	F	EF
1877CC	210.00	400.00
1877S	125.00	175.00
1878 proof only	—	1,250.00
1878CC	675.00	1,750.00
1878S	125.00	175.00
1879 proof only	—	950.00
1880 proof only	—	950.00
1881 proof only	—	1,000.00
1882 proof only	—	1,000.00
1883 proof only	—	1,200.00
1884 proof only	—	10 known
1885 proof only	—	five known

MORGAN DOLLARS

The Morgan dollar was introduced as a result of pressure from the silver-mining lobby. For decades, silver dollars had been scarce in circulation. With the boom in silver mining, the price of the metal dropped as more became available. Something needed to be done to remove the excess silver from the market.

The new design coincided with the reintroduction of the silver dollar. Because they were inconvenient, however, many, perhaps hundreds of thousands, of these dollars sat for decades in bags, held as private, bank, and government reserves. The U.S. Treasury was stuck with such an excess that thousands remained on hand for almost a century, prompting the famous GSA auction of silver dollars in the 1970s. Those coins in distinctive GSA cases often command a slight premium.

Artistically, many consider the Morgan dollar, named after its designer, George T. Morgan, an aesthetically pleasing but unoriginal design. Morgan's competence (and perhaps his interesting use of Gothic script) may perhaps be attributed to his training at the Royal Mint in London. A long gap exists between 1904 and the last Morgan issue in 1921. During this time, the master dies were lost and new ones had to be prepared. As a result, there are subtle differences of relief in the 1921 issue. It is less pleasing and dealer "bids" are often less for that year than for other bulk Morgan dollars. Another subtle variation in the appearance of Morgan dollars is the variation in quality of strike from mint to mint. San Francisco-made examples are usually fully struck, Philadelphia are medium, and New Orleans dollars are usually the most weakly struck. The eagle's breast on high-grade pieces is usually the spot where these differences are most obvious.

Morgans have been among the most popular coins to invest in. This is partially due to their availability in great quantities in uncirculated condition, the typical grade favored by investment promoters and the mass of investors. It is ironic that their sheer commonness has contributed to their desirability.

Known Counterfeits: Genuine coins have been known altered to pass for 1879CC, 1889CC, 1892S, 1893S, 1894, 1895, 1895S, 1896S, 1901, 1903S and 1904S dates. Cast counterfeits are known of 1878, 1878S, 1879S, 1880O, 1881, 1883, 1883S, 1885, 1888O, 1889, 1889O, 1892O, 1899O, 1901, 1902, 1903, 1904S, 1921D and 1921S. Struck counterfeits of certain rare dates are also possible. Cleaned coins are common and are heavily discounted, as are scuffed and heavily edge-knocked pieces. Be careful to avoid coins with false toning.

	VF	MS-60
1878, 8 tail feathers	25.00	125.00
1878, 7 over 8 tail feathers	22.00	115.00
1878, 7 feathers	20.00	56.00
1878, 7 feathers, rev. of 1879	19.00	67.00
1878CC	95.00	220.00
1878S	19.50	46.00
1879	18.00	30.00
1879CC	145.00	2,650.00
1879O	18.00	72.00
1879S	18.00	40.00

	VF	MS-60
1880	18.00	30.00
1880CC	115.00	480.00
1880O	18.00	60.00
1880S	18.00	33.00
1881	18.00	30.00
1881CC	300.00	500.00
1881O	18.00	30.00
1881S	18.00	30.00
1882	18.00	30.00
1882CC	95.00	215.00
1882O	18.00	32.50
1882O, O over S	30.00	170.00
1882S	18.00	33.00
1883	18.00	30.00
1883CC	100.00	210.00
1883O	18.00	30.00
1883S	18.00	490.00
1884	18.00	30.00
1884CC	95.00	205.00

1881CC Morgan Dollar

	VF	MS-60
1884O	18.00	30.00
1884S	18.50	4,100.00
1885	18.50	30.00
1885CC	375.00	560.00
1885O	18.50	30.00
1885S	27.50	185.00
1886	18.50	30.00
1886O	18.50	505.00
1886S	48.50	240.00
1887, 7 over 6	33.00	250.00
1887	18.00	30.00
1887O, 7 over 6	30.00	350.00
1887O	18.00	54.00
1887S	18.50	100.00
1888	18.50	30.00
1888O	18.00	30.00
1888S	80.00	240.00
1889	18.50	30.00
1889CC	1,700.00	17,500.00

1887O Morgan Dollar

	VF	MS-60
1889O	18.00	140.00
1889S	55.00	200.00
1890	18.00	30.00
1890CC	94.00	350.00
1890O	18.00	56.00
1890S	18.00	56.00
1891	18.00	51.00
1891CC	95.00	345.00
1891O	18.00	135.00
1891S	18.00	60.00
1892	18.50	150.00
1892CC	160.00	825.00
1892O	19.50	100.00
1892S	46.00	34,000.00
1893	140.00	540.00
1893CC	335.00	3,130.00
1893O	230.00	1,500.00
1893S	5,000.00	75,000.00

1892S Morgan Dollar

	VF	MS-60
1894	1,250.00	3,200.00
1894O	57.50	550.00
1894S	68.50	570.00
1895 proof only	—	22,000.00
1895O	340.00	13,000.00
1895S	335.00	2,250.00
1896	18.00	30.00
1896O	18.50	940.00
1896S	47.50	1,250.00
1897	18.00	30.00
1897O	18.50	650.00
1897S	18.50	56.00
1898	18.50	30.00
1898O	18.50	30.00
1898S	22.50	260.00
1899	54.00	125.00
1899O	18.50	30.00
1899S	25.00	325.00

	VF	MS-60
1900	18.00	30.00
1900O	18.00	32.00
1900O, O over CC	34.00	230.00
1900S	19.50	245.00
1901	30.00	1,800.00
1901O	18.00	32.00
1901S	29.00	340.00
1902	18.00	42.50
1902O	18.00	30.00
1902S	100.00	375.00
1903	50.00	67.50
1903O	250.00	400.00
1903S	100.00	3,800.00
1904	20.00	80.00
1904O	20.00	33.00
1904S	50.00	990.00
1921	12.50	19.50
1921D	12.50	40.00
1921S	12.50	30.00

1901 Morgan Dollar

PEACE DOLLARS

Like the Morgan dollar before it, the Peace dollar was the result of Congressional authorization for a new large coinage of silver dollars. When the famous numismatist Farran Zerbe learned that this new issue of dollars was to bear the old Morgan design, he agitated for a new, artistically more progressive replacement. This was to be a new radiant Liberty head by sculptor Anthony de Francisci. It was not only in harmony with the new designs for the other denominations, especially those by Weinman and St. Gaudens, but also commemorated the end of World War I. The word PEACE can be seen upon the rocky perch on which the eagle stands.

The very first Peace Dollars, those struck in 1921 only, were struck in a much higher relief. Later issues have a lower relief more suitable to mass production. The old silver dollar was last made for circulation in 1935. The Peace dollar outlived this death sentence for 30 years in the form of the mysterious issue of 1964. While none have been officially verified, there have long been rumors, generally accepted by the numismatic community, that several escaped the mint's melting pot.

Like the Morgan dollar, this coin is available in mint-state in abundant quantities. The broad smooth surfaces, however, permit many mint-state pieces to reveal unsightly bruises and bag marks.

Known Counterfeits: 1928 altered from 1923 or 1928S, as well as other counterfeits of this date.

	VF	MS-60
1921	92.00	210.00
1922	10.00	16.00
1922D	10.00	24.00
1922S	10.00	23.00
1923	10.00	16.00
1923D	10.50	53.00
1923S	10.50	28.00
1924	10.00	16.00
1924S	31.00	195.00
1925	10.00	16.00
1925S	20.00	75.00
1926	15.00	34.00
1926D	15.00	60.00
1926S	14.00	40.00
1927	31.50	70.00
1927D	21.50	145.00
1927S	28.50	135.00
1928	425.00	500.00
1928S	32.50	140.00

1921 Peace Dollar

	VF	MS-60
1934	21.50	105.00
1934D	19.50	110.00
1934S	45.00	1,700.00
1935	21.50	62.00
1935S	16.50	250.00

1964D no confirmed examples
known

EISENHOWER DOLLARS

The "Ike" dollar was struck as much to commemorate the first manned moon landing in 1969, as to honor President Dwight D. Eisenhower. The reverse of this coin was an adaptation of the Apollo XI insignia, depicting an eagle clutching an olive branch and landing on the moon. The obverse shows a left-facing portrait of Eisenhower.

Circulation strikes were of the same cupro-nickel clad composition as the dime and quarter. Special collectors' issues were also struck in a silver clad version similar to the alloy used for the half dollars of 1965-1970. These special silver coins bearing the "S" mint mark were released in blue envelopes for the uncirculated issues, and brown boxes for the proofs. Most dealers and collectors require that they be in the original packaging.

A special reverse was used to commemorate the bicentennial. It featured the Liberty Bell superimposed on the moon, as arranged by design contest winner Dennis R. Williams. While all bicentennial dollars are dated "1776-1976," they were struck in both 1975 and 1976. The reverse of the former year uses heavy block lettering, the latter mostly used slightly finer letters. They are easily identified by the lack of copper on the reeded edge.

Known Counterfeits: Poor quality counterfeits have recently come out of Communist China. Specifically 1976D is known.

	MS-63	PF
1971	—	3.75
1971D	—	2.25
1971S Silver	6.00	7.00
1972	—	2.75
1972D	—	2.25
1972S Silver	6.50	7.00
1973	—	11.00
1973D	—	11.00
1973S proof only	—	11.00
1973S Silver	8.50	30.00
1974	—	3.00

1974 Eisenhower Dollar

	MS-63	PF
1974D	—	2.75
1974S proof only	—	6.50
1974S Silver	7.50	7.25

Bicentennial Reverse	MS-63	PF
1976 block letters	—	6.00
1976 finer letters	—	2.00
1976D block letters	—	3.25
1976D finer letters	—	2.00
1976S block letters proof only	—	6.00
1976S finer letters proof only	—	6.00
1976S Silver, block letters	14.00	13.00

Regular Issue Continued	MS-63	PF
1977	—	4.25
1977D	—	3.25
1977S proof only	—	8.00
1978	—	2.75
1978D	—	3.00
1978S proof only	—	10.00

1976D Eisenhower Dollar with Bicentennial on Reverse

SUSAN B. ANTHONY DOLLARS

The Anthony "mini-dollar" was struck to achieve two specific ends. It was intended to save the government money, by replacing the quickly worn out one-dollar bill with a coin that would last in circulation for decades. It was also a coin greatly supported and pushed for by the vending machine lobby. The large Ike dollars were inconvenient for vending machines, but a coin of its value was necessary to facilitate the sale of more expensive items in such machines.

Its obverse depicts Frank Gasparro's portrait of Susan B. Anthony, who was instrumental in gaining women the right to vote. The reverse design is the same Apollo XI motif as on the Eisenhower dollar.

Certainly one of the least popular coins in the history of the United States, it was far too close in diameter to the quarter, with which it was frequently confused. It was of the same clad composition. The third year of issue was not even placed into circulation, and was just obtainable in mint sets. The final year was only struck in anticipation of its immediate replacement by the Sacagawea dollar.

Known Counterfeits: Not common.

1979S Susan B. Anthony Dollar with Filled S Mint Mark

	MS-63	PF
1979P narrow rim, far date	—	2.00
1979P wide rim, near date	—	12.00
1979D	—	1.75
1979S	—	2.00
1979S filled S	—	8.00
1979S clear S	—	100.00
1980	—	2.00
1980D	—	2.00
1980S	2.00	8.00
1981	—	6.00
1981D	—	6.00
1981S	—	6.00
1981S filled S	—	8.00
1981S clear S	—	220.00
1999P	1.75	9.50
1999D	—	1.75

SACAGAWEA DOLLARS

Despite the failure of the SBA to win any amount of popular acceptance at all, the reasons why it was originally issued remained. The government could save millions by replacing the dollar bill with a more durable coin. Also, a dollar coin of moderate size was still sought by the vending machine industry to facilitate the sale of more expensive items.

The confusion caused by the Anthony dollar was eliminated by changing the color, and giving the new coin a broad border. This new, well-designed coin depicts Sacagawea, the Shoshone Indian guide and translator who accompanied the Lewis and Clark Expedition to explore the Northwest (1804-06). She carries her infant son on her back. It is the work of Glenna Goodacre. The reverse, designed by Thomas D. Rogers, Jr., depicts a graceful eagle in flight.

While it is the same size as the Anthony dollar, it has a unique composition. It is a brass of 77 percent copper, 12 percent zinc, 7 percent manganese, and 4 percent nickel, bonded to a pure copper core. This coin is prone to spotting. Mint-state examples lacking spots are more desirable.

Known Counterfeits: Quantities are known, primarily made for circulation in Ecuador.

	MS-63	PF
2000P	—	2.00
2000D	—	2.00
2000S	—	10.00
2001P	—	4.00
2001D	—	4.00
2001S	—	40.00
2002P	—	2.00
2002D	—	2.00
2002S	—	26.00
2003P	—	2.50
2003D	—	2.50
2003S	—	12.00

2002D Sacagawea Dollar

2-1/2 DOLLAR GOLD PIECES

The first strikes of the quarter eagle (gold 2-1/2 dollar piece) came the year following the first introduction of American gold coinage, the half eagle and eagle preceding it in 1795. However, it preceded the other denominations as being the first coin to depict the heraldic eagle bearing a shield on its chest, which later was featured on all denominations other than copper.

Its first obverse features a bust of Liberty wearing a tall conical cap, traditionally but inaccurately referred to by numismatists as a turban. This first bust by Robert Scott was replaced by one designed by John Reich, and had a smaller cap. A reverse eagle similar, but more realistic, was paired with our new obverse. A large gap in the striking of quarter eagles followed immediately upon the release of this new design, which was finally restored on the same standard but at a slightly smaller diameter in 1821.

Through most of its history until the 1830s, the quarter eagle was plagued by mass meltings, because it was undervalued relative to its gold content, particularly by European standards. In 1834, this was remedied by reducing the coin's gold content. This was indicated to the public by the removal of the motto over the eagle on the reverse, and by a new capless Liberty head, the "Classic Head" by William Kneass.

The final Coronet-type Liberty head design was a rendition by Christian Gobrecht, which continued in use from 1840 to 1907 without change. Those 1848 pieces countermarked CAL. were struck with gold shipped east by the military governor of California.

In 1908, as part of the same coin design beautification program that later introduced the Walking Liberty half dollar and St. Gaudens double eagle, sculptor Bela Lyon Pratt was asked to prepare new designs for the quarter and half eagle in secret under the authority of President Theodore Roosevelt. His work showed the bust of an Indian chief on the obverse and an eagle with closed wings on the reverse. It was both controversial and innovative in that it bore its design in relief, but recessed below the surface of the coin. While some criticized it both for aesthetic reasons and for fear of it spreading germs in dirt trapped in the recesses, it proved to be a very successful method of shielding the design from wear.

Known Counterfeits: Examples of 1848 CAL, 1875, and 1911D exist made by altering genuine coins of other dates or mints. Struck counterfeits exist of virtually every date in this series. All examples of 1905S are counterfeit—no real ones exist. Be cautious of false C mint marks altered by cutting down an authentic O mint mark. Beware of traces of solder on earlier coins from use as jewelry. Look for interruption in the pattern of edge reeding. Be cautious of cleaned coins. This is harder to detect on gold, which usually does not tone naturally.

1834 2-1/2 Dollar Gold Piece with Classic Head (No Motto)

Classic Head (No Motto)	F	XF
1834	250.00	465.00
1835	250.00	465.00
1836	250.00	465.00
1837	250.00	650.00
1838	250.00	465.00
1838C	850.00	2,000.00
1839	250.00	650.00
1839C	850.00	2,200.00
1839D	850.00	2,800.00
1839O	365.00	925.00

Coronet Type (No Motto)	F	EF
1840	150.00	850.00
1840C	825.00	1,600.00
1840D	1,200.00	8,000.00
1840O	225.00	800.00
1841	—	87,500.00
1841C	675.00	1,600.00
1841D	990.00	3,850.00
1842	450.00	2,900.00

1842O 2-1/2 Dollar Gold Piece with Coronet (No Motto)

Coronet Type (No Motto)	F	EF
1842C	700.00	2,800.00
1842D	900.00	3,350.00
1842O	220.00	1,100.00
1843	150.00	220.00
1843C, crosslet 4, small date	1,100.00	5,000.00
1843C, plain 4, large date	600.00	1,600.00
1843D	700.00	1,850.00
1843O, crosslet 4, small date	150.00	250.00
1843O, plain 4, large date	200.00	450.00
1844	225.00	850.00
1844C	600.00	1,850.00
1844D	650.00	1,850.00
1845	180.00	300.00
1845D	725.00	1,850.00
1845O	525.00	2,000.00
1846	200.00	500.00
1846C	750.00	3,500.00
1846D	700.00	1,850.00
1846O	170.00	400.00

Coronet Type (No Motto)	F	EF
1847	140.00	360.00
1847C	700.00	1,600.00
1847D	700.00	1,850.00
1847O	150.00	375.00
1848	315.00	850.00
1848 CAL. Quarter eagles with CAL over the eagle were struck with gold shipped to the Dept. of War by the governor of California.	6,500.00	24,000.00
1848C	600.00	1,650.00
1848D	700.00	1,850.00
1849	200.00	475.00
1849C	700.00	1,750.00
1849D	700.00	1,850.00
1850	140.00	215.00
1850C	700.00	1,650.00
1850D	700.00	1,850.00
1850O	160.00	450.00
1851	135.00	200.00

1852D 2-1/2 Dollar Gold Piece with Coronet (No Motto)

Coronet Type (No Motto)	F	EF
1851C	700.00	1,650.00
1851D	700.00	1,850.00
1851O	140.00	220.00
1852	135.00	200.00
1852C	700.00	1,750.00
1852D	750.00	2,250.00
1852O	150.00	300.00
1853	135.00	200.00
1853D	950.00	3,200.00
1854	135.00	200.00
1854C	700.00	2,000.00
1854D	1,800.00	5,000.00
1854O	140.00	215.00
1854S	32,500.00	80,000.00
1855	135.00	200.00
1855C	775.00	3,000.00
1855D	2,000.00	7,500.00
1856	135.00	200.00
1856C	700.00	2,200.00

1859 2-1/2 Dollar Gold Piece with Coronet (No Motto)

Coronet Type (No Motto)	F	EF
1856D	3,510.00	9,850.00
1856O	150.00	700.00
1856S	145.00	360.00
1857	135.00	200.00
1857D	700.00	2,500.00
1857O	145.00	350.00
1857S	145.00	330.00
1858	135.00	235.00
1858C	700.00	1,600.00
1859	135.00	250.00
1859D	990.00	3,000.00
1859S	180.00	900.00
1860	135.00	250.00
1860C	700.00	1,800.00
1860S	160.00	675.00
1861	135.00	200.00
1861S	175.00	900.00
1862, 2 over 1	450.00	1,800.00
1862	145.00	300.00

1875 2-1/2 Dollar Gold Piece with Coronet (No Motto)

Coronet Type (No Motto)	F	EF
1862S	400.00	2,100.00
1863 proof only	—	20,000.00
1863S	300.00	1,500.00
1864	2,500.00	11,000.00
1865	2,400.00	7,300.00
1865S	150.00	610.00
1866	650.00	3,500.00
1866S	170.00	650.00
1867	185.00	795.00
1867S	150.00	600.00
1868	170.00	400.00
1868S	135.00	350.00
1869	150.00	450.00
1869S	135.00	440.00
1870	150.00	400.00
1870S	135.00	400.00
1871	150.00	325.00
1871S	135.00	280.00
1872	200.00	750.00

Coronet Type (No Motto)	F	EF
1872S	135.00	400.00
1873 closed 3	135.00	200.00
1873 open 3	135.00	195.00
1873S	135.00	400.00
1874	150.00	365.00
1875	1,750.00	5,000.00
1875S	135.00	300.00
1876	160.00	640.00
1876S	145.00	500.00
1877	250.00	700.00
1877S	135.00	195.00
1878	135.00	195.00
1878S	135.00	195.00
1879	135.00	195.00
1879S	135.00	275.00
1880	160.00	335.00
1881	850.00	2,750.00
1882	150.00	290.00
1883	150.00	440.00

Coronet Type (No Motto)	F	EF
1884	150.00	400.00
1885	400.00	1,700.00
1886	150.00	260.00
1887	150.00	245.00
1888	140.00	225.00
1889	150.00	200.00
1890	150.00	225.00
1891	150.00	200.00
1892	155.00	235.00
1893	145.00	190.00
1894	155.00	230.00
1895	135.00	205.00
1896	135.00	195.00
1897	135.00	195.00
1898	135.00	195.00
1899	135.00	195.00
1900	135.00	250.00
1901	135.00	195.00
1902	135.00	195.00

Coronet Type (No Motto)	F	EF
1903	135.00	195.00
1904	135.00	195.00
1905	135.00	195.00
1906	135.00	195.00
1907	135.00	195.00

Indian Head Type	VF	AU
1908	160.00	190.00
1909	160.00	190.00
1910	160.00	190.00
1911	160.00	190.00
1911D	700.00	2,200.00
1912	160.00	190.00
1913	160.00	190.00
1914	160.00	200.00
1914D	160.00	190.00
1915	160.00	190.00
1925D	160.00	190.00
1926	160.00	190.00
1927	160.00	190.00

1911D 2-1/2 Dollar Gold Piece with Indian Head

Indian Head Type	VF	AU
1928	160.00	190.00
1929	160.00	190.00

5 DOLLAR GOLD PIECES

The first American gold coin to be struck was the half eagle, or $5 gold piece, in 1795. Its first obverse features a bust of Liberty wearing a tall conical cap traditionally, but inaccurately, referred to by numismatists as a turban. Originally this was paired with a reverse design featuring a skinny eagle similar to that on the first dollars, but instead of standing within a wreath, it is seen holding one above its head. As with the other denominations, this was replaced by a plumper heraldic eagle bearing a shield on its chest, which later was featured on all denominations other than copper.

The original bust by Robert Scott was replaced in 1807 by one designed by John Reich, and was wearing a smaller cap. A reverse eagle similar, but more realistic, was paired with the new obverse. While the design and net gold content did not change for almost 30 years, the coin's diameter was at first increased and then reduced.

Through most of its history until the 1830s, the half eagle was plagued by mass meltings, being undervalued relative to its gold content, particularly by European standards. In 1834, this was remedied by reducing the coin's gold content. This was indicated to the public by the removal of the motto over the eagle on the reverse, and by a new capless Liberty head, the "Classic Head" by William Kneass. The final Coronet-type Liberty head design was a rendition by Christian Gobrecht, which continued in use from 1839 to 1908, the motto being replaced over the eagle in 1866.

In 1908, as part of the same coin design beautification program that later introduced the Walking Liberty half dollar and St. Gaudens double eagle, sculptor Bela Lyon Pratt was asked to prepare new designs for the quarter and half eagle in secret under the authority of President Theodore Roosevelt. His work showed the bust of an Indian chief on the obverse and an eagle with closed wings on the reverse. It was both controversial and innovative in that it bore its design in relief, but recessed below the surface of the coin. While some criticized it both for aesthetic reasons and for fear of it spreading germs in dirt trapped in the recesses, it proved to be a very successful method of shielding the design from wear.

Known Counterfeits: 1811, 1815 (altered), 1841O (probable), 1852C, 1854S (altered), 1858, 1870CC (altered), 1875, 1877 (altered), 1885, 1885S, 1887 Proof (altered), 1892, 1892O (altered), 1906S, 1907D, 1908 (Liberty), 1908D, 1909 Matte Proof, 1909D, 1909O,

1910D, 1914D, 1914S, and 1915D (all counterfeit), among others. Be cautious of false C mint marks altered by cutting down an authentic O mint mark. Beware of traces of solder on earlier coins used as jewelry. Look for interruption in the pattern of edge reeding. Be cautious of cleaned coins. This is harder to detect on gold, which usually does not tone naturally.

Classic Head (No Motto)	VF	EF
1834 plain 4	370.00	540.00
1834 crosslet 4	1,600.00	2,600.00
1835	370.00	550.00
1836	370.00	540.00
1837	370.00	570.00
1838	370.00	540.00
1838C	1,850.00	3,850.00
1838D	1,450.00	3,400.00

Coronet Type (No Motto)	VF	EF
1839	275.00	480.00
1839C	2,000.00	3,000.00
1839D	1,600.00	2,300.00

1834 5 Dollar Gold Piece with
Classic Head and Crosslet 4 (No Motto)

1841 5 Dollar Gold Piece with Coronet (No Motto)

Coronet Type (No Motto)	VF	EF
1840	235.00	360.00
1840C	2,000.00	2,900.00
1840D	1,500.00	3,000.00
1840O	325.00	850.00
1841	375.00	1,750.00
1841C	1,400.00	1,900.00
1841D	1,450.00	1,900.00
1841O	—	two known
1842 small letters	345.00	1,100.00
1842 large letters	750.00	2,000.00
1842C small date	9,000.00	23,000.00
1842C large date	1,400.00	2,000.00
1842D small letters	1,450.00	1,900.00
1842D large letters	2,200.00	5,800.00
1842O	1,000.00	3,000.00
1843	210.00	250.00
1843C	1,400.00	1,900.00
1843D	1,450.00	1,900.00
1843O small letters	500.00	1,800.00

Coronet Type (No Motto)	VF	EF
1843O large letters	250.00	1,125.00
1844	220.00	240.00
1844C	1,400.00	3,000.00
1844D	1,450.00	1,900.00
1844O	250.00	375.00
1845	220.00	240.00
1845D	1,450.00	1,900.00
1845O	410.00	750.00
1846 small date	220.00	240.00
1846	220.00	240.00
1846C	1,450.00	2,900.00
1846D	1,450.00	1,900.00
1846O	200.00	375.00
1847	220.00	250.00
1847C	1,400.00	1,900.00
1847D	1,450.00	1,900.00
1847O	4,700.00	8,000.00
1848	225.00	275.00
1848C	1,400.00	1,900.00

1851 5 Dollar Gold Piece with Coronet (No Motto)

Coronet Type (No Motto)	VF	EF
1848D	1,450.00	1,900.00
1849	220.00	270.00
1849C	1,400.00	1,900.00
1849D	1,450.00	1,900.00
1850	275.00	600.00
1850C	1,400.00	1,900.00
1850D	1,450.00	1,900.00
1851	220.00	240.00
1851C	1,400.00	1,900.00
1851D	1,450.00	1,900.00
1851O	565.00	1,500.00
1852	220.00	245.00
1852C	1,400.00	1,900.00
1852D	1,450.00	1,900.00
1853	220.00	240.00
1853C	1,400.00	1,900.00
1853D	1,450.00	1,900.00
1854	220.00	250.00
1854C	1,400.00	1,900.00

Coronet Type (No Motto)	VF	EF
1854D	1,450.00	1,900.00
1854O	300.00	525.00
1854S	—	extremely rare
1855	220.00	235.00
1855C	1,400.00	2,000.00
1855D	1,450.00	1,900.00
1855O	650.00	2,100.00
1855S	390.00	975.00
1856	220.00	240.00
1856C	1,400.00	1,900.00
1856D	1,450.00	1,900.00
1856O	650.00	1,250.00
1856S	300.00	625.00
1857	220.00	240.00
1857C	1,400.00	1,900.00
1857D	1,450.00	1,900.00
1857O	640.00	1,400.00
1857S	300.00	525.00

1858 5 Dollar Gold Piece with Coronet (No Motto)

Coronet Type (No Motto)	VF	EF
1858	240.00	550.00
1858C	1,400.00	1,900.00
1858D	1,450.00	1,900.00
1858S	700.00	2,350.00
1859	325.00	625.00
1859C	1,400.00	1,900.00
1859D	1,450.00	1,900.00
1859S	1,250.00	3,500.00
1860	275.00	575.00
1860C	1,400.00	2,200.00
1860D	1,450.00	2,000.00
1860S	1,100.00	2,100.00
1861	220.00	245.00
1861C	1,850.00	3,900.00
1861D	4,400.00	7,000.00
1861S	1,000.00	4,500.00
1862	700.00	1,850.00
1862S	3,000.00	6,300.00
1863	1,200.00	3,750.00

Coronet Type (No Motto)	VF	EF
1863S	1,450.00	3,900.00
1864	630.00	1,850.00
1864S	6,000.00	16,000.00
1865	1,300.00	4,100.00
1865S	1,350.00	2,400.00
1866S	1,650.00	4,000.00

Coronet Type (With Motto)	VF	EF
1866	800.00	1,650.00
1866S	900.00	2,600.00
1867	500.00	1,600.00
1867S	1,300.00	2,700.00
1868	650.00	1,000.00
1868S	400.00	1,550.00
1869	925.00	2,300.00
1869S	500.00	1,750.00
1870	800.00	1,950.00
1870CC	5,000.00	13,000.00
1870S	950.00	2,600.00

1866 5 Dollar Gold Piece with Coronet and Motto

Coronet Type (With Motto)	VF	EF
1871	950.00	1,800.00
1871CC	1,100.00	3,3000.00
1871S	500.00	1,000.00
1872	850.00	1,900.00
1872CC	1,100.00	4,800.00
1872S	445.00	800.00
1873 closed 3	180.00	225.00
1873 open 3	180.00	215.00
1873CC	2,250.00	12,500.00
1873S	510.00	1,400.00
1874	650.00	1,650.00
1874CC	800.00	1,750.00
1874S	650.00	2,000.00
1875	34,000.00	45,000.00
1875CC	1,400.00	4,400.00
1875S	675.00	2,250.00
1876	1,000.00	2,400.00
1876CC	1,200.00	5,000.00
1876S	2,000.00	3,600.00

Coronet Type (With Motto)	VF	EF
1877	900.00	2,700.00
1877CC	1,000.00	3,300.00
1877S	390.00	650.00
1878	160.00	190.00
1878CC	3,000.00	7,300.00
1878S	165.00	190.00
1879	165.00	180.00
1879CC	525.00	1,400.00
1879S	180.00	225.00
1880	160.00	175.00
1880CC	425.00	770.00
1880S	160.00	175.00
1881 1 over 0	330.00	600.00
1881	160.00	175.00
1881CC	515.00	1,400.00
1881S	160.00	175.00
1882	160.00	175.00
1882CC	380.00	545.00
1882S	160.00	175.00

1884S 5 Dollar Gold Piece with Coronet and Motto

Coronet Type (With Motto)	VF	EF
1883	160.00	175.00
1883CC	450.00	990.00
1883S	195.00	240.00
1884	170.00	200.00
1884CC	550.00	975.00
1884S	170.00	200.00
1885	160.00	175.00
1885S	160.00	175.00
1886	160.00	175.00
1886S	160.00	175.00
1887 proof only	—	130,000.00
1887S	160.00	175.00
1888	175.00	220.00
1888S	175.00	200.00
1889	280.00	440.00
1890	385.00	475.00
1890CC	320.00	385.00
1891	170.00	200.00
1891CC	310.00	410.00

Coronet Type (With Motto)	VF	EF
1892	160.00	175.00
1892CC	310.00	390.00
1892O	500.00	990.00
1892S	180.00	195.00
1893	160.00	175.00
1893CC	310.00	440.00
1893O	215.00	310.00
1893S	170.00	200.00
1894	160.00	175.00
1894O	200.00	350.00
1894S	230.00	365.00
1895	160.00	175.00
1895S	200.00	275.00
1896	160.00	175.00
1896S	200.00	250.00
1897	160.00	175.00
1897S	175.00	210.00
1898	160.00	175.00
1898S	175.00	200.00

Coronet Type (With Motto)	VF	EF
1899	160.00	175.00
1899S	170.00	180.00
1900	160.00	175.00
1900S	170.00	190.00
1901	160.00	175.00
1901S 1 over 0	165.00	200.00
1901S	160.00	175.00
1902	160.00	175.00
1902S	160.00	175.00
1903	160.00	175.00
1903S	160.00	175.00
1904	160.00	175.00
1904S	175.00	215.00
1905	160.00	175.00
1905S	170.00	190.00
1906	160.00	175.00
1906D	160.00	175.00
1906S	165.00	185.00
1907	160.00	175.00

1899 5 Dollar Gold Piece with Coronet and Motto

Coronet Type (With Motto)	VF	EF
1907D	160.00	175.00
1908	160.00	175.00

Indian Head Type	VF	EF
1908	195.00	220.00
1908D	195.00	220.00
1908S	195.00	435.00
1909	195.00	220.00
1909D	195.00	220.00
1909O	650.00	2,000.00
1909S	195.00	270.00
1910	195.00	220.00
1910D	195.00	220.00
1910S	195.00	280.00
1911	195.00	220.00
1911D	350.00	450.00
1911S	195.00	270.00
1912	195.00	220.00
1912S	195.00	320.00

1908 5 Dollar Gold Piece with Indian Head

Indian Head Type	VF	EF
1913	195.00	220.00
1913S	200.00	290.00
1914	195.00	220.00
1914D	195.00	230.00
1914S	260.00	300.00
1915	195.00	220.00
1915S	270.00	400.00
1916S	260.00	295.00
1929	2,750.00	5,500.00

10 DOLLAR GOLD PIECES

Among the first two American gold coins to be struck was the eagle or $10 gold piece in 1795, and it was George Washington himself who received the first example. Its first obverse features a bust of Liberty by Robert Scot, wearing a tall conical cap traditionally, but inaccurately, referred to by numismatists as a turban. Originally this was paired with a reverse design featuring a skinny eagle similar to that on the first silver dollars, but instead of standing within a wreath, it is seen holding one above its head. As with the other denominations, this was replaced by a plumper heraldic eagle bearing a shield on its chest, which later was featured on all denominations other than copper.

All these early eagles were struck on a primitive screw press with hand engraved dies, no two of which were identical. Many will show evidence of adjustment marks, a scraping of metal from the blank before striking to prevent the coin from being overweight. While not desirable, they are not considered damage, as they are part of the manufacturing process.

The initial issue of 1795-1804 was plagued by mass meltings and wholesale export, being undervalued relative to its gold content, particularly by European standards. As a result, its coinage was completely suspended for more than 30 years.

It was reintroduced in 1838 on the reduced gold standard adopted in 1834 to prevent these abuses. The new gold eagle featured a Liberty head wearing a coronet, Christian Gobrecht's interpretation of a painting of Venus by Benjamin West. A new, more realistic reverse eagle still wore a heraldic shield. This design continued in use until 1907, the motto being replaced over the eagle in 1866.

In 1908, as part of the same coin design beautification trend that later introduced the Walking Liberty half dollar and Mercury dime, President Theodore Roosevelt asked noted sculptor Augustus St. Gaudens to prepare new designs for the eagle and double eagle. HIs work showed the head of Liberty wearing an Indian warbonnet, the headdress being added, at the President's instruction, to St. Gauden's head originally designed as Victory. The reverse featured a proud eagle with closed wings.

As Roosevelt believed the use of the motto "In G-d We Trust" on coinage to be a debased use of the divine name, it was omitted from the initial issues. This upset Congress so much that a law was enacted that restored it during 1908.

Known Counterfeits: 1799, 1858 (altered), 1889 (altered from Ps), 1901S, 1906D, 1906S, 1907, 1908 with Motto Proof, 1908S, 1909 Matte Proof, 1909S, 1910 Proof, 1910S, 1911 Proof, 1911D, 1911S, 1912S, 1913, 1913S, 1914S, 1915S, 1916S, 1926, 1932, 1933, among others, especially 1870 to 1933. Be cautious of false C mint marks altered by cutting down an authentic O mint mark. Beware of traces of solder on earlier coins used as jewelry. Look for interruption in the pattern of edge reeding. Be cautious of cleaned coins. This is harder to detect on gold, which usually does not tone naturally.

Coronet Type (No Motto)	VF	EF
1838	1,100.00	2,900.00
1839 large letters	1,000.00	1,900.00
1839 small letters	1,500.00	3,500.00
1840	400.00	650.00

1849O 10 Dollar Gold Piece with Coronet (No Motto)

Coronet Type (No Motto)	VF	EF
1841	385.00	500.00
1841O	2,200.00	5,000.00
1842 small date	375.00	620.00
1842 large date	325.00	475.00
1842O	370.00	510.00
1843	370.00	490.00
1843O	370.00	470.00
1844	1,350.00	2,700.00
1844O	325.00	475.00
1845	600.00	775.00
1845O	380.00	650.00
1846	625.00	900.00
1846O	425.00	770.00
1847	300.00	350.00
1847O	325.00	375.00
1848	340.00	375.00
1848O	525.00	1,050.00
1849	300.00	350.00
1849O	710.00	2,000.00

Coronet Type (No Motto)	VF	EF
1850 large date	300.00	380.00
1850 small date	325.00	450.00
1850O	380.00	875.00
1851	320.00	470.00
1851O	315.00	440.00
1852	300.00	350.00
1852O	650.00	1,100.00
1853 3 over 2	550.00	750.00
1853	300.00	350.00
1853O	325.00	485.00
1854	320.00	400.00
1854O small date	375.00	675.00
1854O large date	475.00	875.00
1854S	325.00	410.00
1855	300.00	350.00
1855O	625.00	1,250.00
1855S	1,250.00	2,200.00
1856	300.00	350.00
1856O	715.00	1,200.00

1862S 10 Dollar Gold Piece with Coronet (No Motto)

Coronet Type (No Motto)	VF	EF
1856S	320.00	500.00
1857	490.00	850.00
1857O	975.00	1,850.00
1857S	375.00	950.00
1858	4,650.00	7,250.00
1858O	435.00	740.00
1858S	1,450.00	3,100.00
1859	390.00	750.00
1859O	3,800.00	8,200.00
1859S	1,800.00	4,500.00
1860	420.00	775.00
1860O	575.00	1,100.00
1860S	3,200.00	6,000.00
1861	300.00	350.00
1861S	1,600.00	2,900.00
1862	525.00	1,000.00
1862S	1,750.00	2,950.00
1863	3,650.00	9,800.00
1863S	1,600.00	3,350.00

Coronet Type (No Motto)	VF	EF
1864	1,600.00	4,000.00
1864S	4,900.00	12,500.00
1865	1,950.00	3,500.00
1865S	5,400.00	10,700.00
1865S 865 over inverted 186	2,800.00	6,100.00
1866S	2,400.00	3,300.00

Coronet Type (With Motto)	VF	EF
1866	775.00	1,650.00
1866S	1,550.00	3,400.00
1867	1,500.00	2,600.00
1867S	2,000.00	5,200.00
1868	500.00	750.00
1868S	1,250.00	2,100.00
1869	1,400.00	2,800.00
1869S	1,500.00	2,500.00
1870	800.00	1,175.00
1870CC	9,250.00	22,500.00
1870S	1,100.00	2,500.00

1873CC 10 Dollar Gold Piece with Coronet and Motto

Coronet Type (With Motto)	VF	EF
1871	1,450.00	2,350.00
1871CC	2,150.00	4,950.00
1871S	1,075.00	1,550.00
1872	2,200.00	3,600.00
1872CC	3,000.00	8,900.00
1872S	550.00	850.00
1873	4,500.00	9,500.00
1873CC	5,000.00	12,000.00
1873S	950.00	1,950.00
1874	255.00	270.00
1874CC	850.00	2,500.00
1874S	1,150.00	3,250.00
1875	38,000.00	53,000.00
1875CC	3,700.00	8,800.00
1876	3,400.00	4,800.00
1876CC	3,200.00	6,500.00
1876S	1,250.00	2,000.00
1877	2,100.00	53800.00
1877CC	2,300.00	4,750.00

Coronet Type (With Motto)	VF	EF
1877S	550.00	700.00
1878	255.00	270.00
1878CC	3,650.00	7,600.00
1878S	425.00	550.00
1879	255.00	270.00
1879CC	7,500.00	13,000.00
1879O	2,300.00	3,750.00
1879S	255.00	270.00
1880	255.00	270.00
1880CC	475.00	700.00
1880O	410.00	700.00
1880S	255.00	270.00
1881	255.00	270.00
1881CC	360.00	515.00
1881O	375.00	650.00
1881S	255.00	270.00
1882	255.00	270.00
1882CC	850.00	1,300.00
1882O	375.00	575.00

1882O 10 Dollar Gold Piece with Coronet and Motto

Coronet Type (With Motto)	VF	EF
1882S	255.00	270.00
1883	255.00	270.00
1883CC	425.00	700.00
1883O	3,000.00	6,800.00
1883S	255.00	270.00
1884	255.00	270.00
1884CC	600.00	950.00
1884S	255.00	270.00
1885	255.00	270.00
1885S	255.00	270.00
1886	255.00	270.00
1886S	255.00	270.00
1887	255.00	270.00
1887S	255.00	270.00
1888	255.00	270.00
1888O	255.00	270.00
1888S	255.00	270.00
1889	500.00	650.00
1889S	255.00	270.00

Coronet Type (With Motto)	VF	EF
1890	255.00	275.00
1890CC	375.00	450.00
1891	255.00	270.00
1891CC	355.00	400.00
1892	255.00	270.00
1892CC	350.00	450.00
1892O	255.00	275.00
1892S	255.00	270.00
1893	255.00	270.00
1893CC	425.00	625.00
1893O	260.00	315.00
1893S	255.00	270.00
1894	255.00	270.00
1894O	255.00	270.00
1894S	265.00	385.00
1895	255.00	270.00
1895O	255.00	270.00
1895S	255.00	300.00
1896	255.00	270.00

1901 10 Dollar Gold Piece with Coronet and Motto

Coronet Type (With Motto)	VF	EF
1896S	255.00	270.00
1897	255.00	270.00
1897O	255.00	270.00
1897S	255.00	270.00
1898	255.00	270.00
1898S	255.00	270.00
1899	255.00	270.00
1899O	255.00	275.00
1899S	255.00	275.00
1900	255.00	270.00
1900S	255.00	275.00
1901	255.00	270.00
1901O	255.00	270.00
1901S	255.00	270.00
1902	255.00	270.00
1902S	255.00	270.00
1903	255.00	270.00
1903O	255.00	270.00
1903S	255.00	270.00

Coronet Type (With Motto)	VF	EF
1904	255.00	270.00
1904O	255.00	270.00
1905	255.00	270.00
1905S	255.00	270.00
1906	255.00	270.00
1906D	255.00	270.00
1906O	255.00	270.00
1906S	255.00	270.00
1907	255.00	270.00
1907D	255.00	270.00
1907S	255.00	270.00

Indian Head/No Motto	VF	EF
1907 wire rim, periods	—	11,000.00
1907 rounded rim, periods	—	24,000.00
1907 no periods	350.00	375.00
1908	350.00	390.00
1908D	335.00	375.00

1907 10 Dollar Gold Piece with Indian Head and No Motto

Indian Head/With Motto	VF	EF
1908	320.00	360.00
1908D	320.00	360.00
1908S	360.00	390.00
1909	320.00	335.00
1909D	320.00	335.00
1909S	330.00	350.00
1910	335.00	375.00
1910D	330.00	365.00
1910S	330.00	370.00
1911	325.00	365.00
1911D	425.00	725.00
1911S	365.00	550.00
1912	330.00	335.00
1912S	330.00	350.00
1913	320.00	335.00
1913S	550.00	640.00
1914	325.00	340.00
1914D	320.00	340.00
1914S	320.00	340.00

1913 10 Dollar Gold Piece with Indian Head and Motto

Indian Head/With Motto	VF	EF
1915	320.00	340.00
1915S	550.00	700.00
1916S	330.00	350.00
1920S	5,000.00	7,250.00
1926	300.00	325.00
1930S	4,000.00	6,000.00
1932	300.00	325.00
1933	MS-60	80,000.00

20 DOLLAR GOLD PIECES

The California Gold Rush of the 1840s resulted in large quantities of bullion being received at the mint for coinage. Partially to make this massive coinage more expedient and partially because of the obvious convenience of using fewer coins for large international payments, the bill proposing the introduction of gold dollars was amended to include a large $20 gold piece called a "double eagle." James B. Longacre engraved a bust of Liberty wearing a coronet similar to, but of much more refined style, than the one in use on smaller gold since 1838. A facing heraldic eagle with a circlet of stars and a radiant arc above graced the reverse, the two motto ribbons at its sides suggesting the denomination of two eagles.

This design continued in use until 1907, the motto being placed within the circlet over the eagle in 1866. Two other minor modifications were attempted. The first (1861), called the Paquet reverse, is a subtle rearrangement of details, and for technical reasons was abandoned almost immediately. The other was the replacement in 1877 of the abbreviation D. with the word dollars.

In 1908, as part of the same coin design beautification trend that later introduced the Walking Liberty half dollar and Mercury dime, President Theodore Roosevelt asked noted sculptor Augustus St. Gaudens to prepare new designs for the double eagle and eagle. His work showed a full figure of Liberty, holding a torch and olive branch, striding towards the viewer. It was very much inspired by Hellenistic sculpture, as correspondence between the two men clearly confirms. The reverse featured an eagle in mid-flight with a rising sun and rays in the background.

As Roosevelt believed the use of the motto "In God We Trust" on coinage to be a debased use of the divine name, it was omitted from the initial issues. This upset Congress so much that a law was enacted replacing it during 1908. To avoid public confusion, the date was changed from Roman numerals to Arabic ones, and because the initial design was of such high relief that it took three strikes by the dies, its relief was lowered as well.

Both the Liberty type and the Saint Gaudens type are often found with heavy bag marks due to their soft metal and heavy weight. Examples virtually free from these marks command a substantial premium.

Known Counterfeits: 1879, 1879O, 1881 (altered), 1882 (altered), 1887 (altered), 1891, 1894, 1897S, 1898S, 1899S, 1900, 1900S, 1901S, 1903, 1903S, 1904, 1904S, 1906, 1906S, MCMVII, 1907 (Saint-Gaudens), 1908, 1909, 1910D, 1910S, 1911D, 1914D, 1914S, 1915, 1916S, 1919, 1920, 1921, 1922, 1923, 1924, 1925, 1926, 1927, 1927D (altered), 1928, 1929, among others, especially 1870 to 1932. Be cautious, as this series has been extensively counterfeited. Beware of traces of solder on earlier coins used as jewelry. Look for interruption in the pattern of edge reeding. Be cautious of cleaned coins. This is harder to detect on gold, which usually does not tone naturally.

Liberty Head—Type I	VF	EF
1849	unique	
1850	700.00	1,150.00
1850O	850.00	1,400.00
1851	650.00	700.00
1851O	800.00	985.00

1850 20 Dollar Gold Piece with Liberty Head (Type I)

Liberty Head—Type I	VF	EF
1852	650.00	720.00
1852O	800.00	1,000.00
1853 3 over 2	700.00	850.00
1853	650.00	720.00
1853O	750.00	1,200.00
1854	650.00	715.00
1854O	30,000.00	57,000.00
1854S	700.00	825.00
1855	650.00	725.00
1855O	2,500.00	5,900.00
1855S	675.00	750.00
1856	675.00	725.00
1856O	42,000.00	75,000.00
1856S	650.00	725.00
1857	650.00	675.00
1857O	1,050.00	1,950.00
1857S	650.00	700.00
1858	700.00	925.00
1858O	1,500.00	2,200.00

Liberty Head—Type I	VF	EF
1858S	650.00	800.00
1859	960.00	2,100.00
1859O	4,000.00	8,000.00
1859S	650.00	700.00
1860	650.00	700.00
1860O	3,800.00	7,500.00
1860S	750.00	900.00
1861	650.00	700.00
1861O Most of these were struck by Louisiana and the Confederacy after withdrawal from the Union.	2,500.00	5,000.00
1861S	650.00	800.00
1861 Paquet rev.	Proof-67	660,000.00
1861S Paquet rev.	11,000.00	22,000.00
1862	925.00	1,450.00
1862S	650.00	900.00
1863	720.00	880.00
1863S	650.00	850.00

Liberty Head—Type I	VF	EF
1864	775.00	990.00
1864S	650.00	750.00
1865	650.00	700.00
1865S	650.00	715.00
1866S	1,950.00	3,500.00

Liberty Head (With Motto)—Type II	VF	EF
1866	650.00	700.00
1866S	600.00	650.00
1867	600.00	650.00
1867S	600.00	650.00
1868	800.00	1,100.00
1868S	600.00	750.00
1869	675.00	850.00
1869S	600.00	650.00
1870	700.00	960.00
1870CC	85,000.00	115,000.00
1870S	600.00	675.00
1871	700.00	900.00

*1869S 20 Dollar Gold Piece
with Liberty Head and Motto (Type II)*

Liberty Head (With Motto)—Type II	VF	EF
1871CC	6,000.00	9,600.00
1871S	600.00	700.00
1872	600.00	700.00
1872CC	1,900.00	2,400.00
1872S	600.00	700.00
1873 closed 3	650.00	750.00
1873 open 3	600.00	650.00
1873CC	2,250.00	3,500.00
1873S	600.00	650.00
1874	600.00	650.00
1874CC	1,100.00	1,500.00
1874S	600.00	650.00
1875	600.00	650.00
1875CC	1,100.00	1,300.00
1875S	600.00	650.00
1876	600.00	650.00
1876CC	1,100.00	1,300.00
1876S	600.00	650.00

Liberty Head—Type III	VF	EF
1877	530.00	560.00
1877CC	1,250.00	1,550.00
1877S	530.00	560.00
1878	530.00	560.00
1878CC	2,000.00	2,800.00
1878S	530.00	560.00
1879	530.00	560.00
1879CC	2,000.00	3,000.00
1879O	4,000.00	6,750.00
1879S	530.00	560.00
1880	530.00	560.00
1880S	530.00	560.00
1881	4,000.00	6,750.00
1881S	530.00	560.00
1882	7,000.00	15,000.00
1882CC	1,150.00	1,375.00
1882S	530.00	560.00
1883	proof only	45,000.00
1883CC	1,100.00	1,250.00

1877 20 Dollar Gold Piece with Liberty Head (Type III)

Liberty Head—Type III	VF	EF
1883S	530.00	560.00
1884	proof only	71,000.00
1884CC	1,100.00	1,300.00
1884S	530.00	560.00
1885	6,000.00	8,000.00
1885CC	2,100.00	3,000.00
1885S	530.00	560.00
1886	7,000.00	11,500.00
1887	proof only	30,000.00
1887S	530.00	560.00
1888	530.00	560.00
1888S	530.00	560.00
1889	600.00	650.00
1889CC	1,250.00	1,450.00
1889S	530.00	560.00
1890	530.00	560.00
1890CC	1,100.00	1,400.00
1890S	530.00	560.00
1891	3,200.00	9,700.00

Liberty Head—Type III	VF	EF
1891CC	3,500.00	5,000.00
1891S	530.00	560.00
1892	1,150.00	1,650.00
1892CC	1,200.00	1,400.00
1892S	530.00	560.00
1893	530.00	560.00
1893CC	1,400.00	1,750.00
1893S	530.00	560.00
1894	530.00	560.00
1894S	530.00	560.00
1895	530.00	560.00
1895S	530.00	560.00
1896	530.00	560.00
1896S	530.00	560.00
1897	530.00	560.00
1897S	530.00	560.00
1898	530.00	560.00
1898S	530.00	560.00
1899	530.00	560.00

1903 20 Dollar Gold Piece with Liberty Head (Type III)

Liberty Head—Type III	VF	EF
1899S	530.00	560.00
1900	530.00	560.00
1900S	530.00	560.00
1901	530.00	560.00
1901S	530.00	560.00
1902	530.00	560.00
1902S	530.00	560.00
1903	530.00	560.00
1903S	530.00	560.00
1904	530.00	560.00
1904S	530.00	560.00
1905	530.00	560.00
1905S	530.00	560.00
1906	530.00	560.00
1906D	530.00	560.00
1906S	530.00	560.00
1907	530.00	560.00
1907D	530.00	560.00
1907S	530.00	560.00

1907 High Relief 20 Dollar
Saint Gaudens Gold Piece with No Motto

Saint-Gaudens/No Motto	VF	EF
1907 high relief, wire rim	6,100.00	6,700.00
1907 high relief, flat rim	6,250.00	6,900.00
1907 Arabic numerals	465.00	485.00
1908	455.00	475.00
1908D	340.00	485.00

Saint-Gaudens/ With Motto	VF	EF
1908	515.00	535.00
1908D	515.00	495.00
1908S	750.00	1,400.00
1909/8	525.00	580.00
1909	515.00	560.00
1909D	515.00	690.00
1909S	515.00	535.00
1910	515.00	535.00
1910D	515.00	535.00
1910S	515.00	535.00
1911	515.00	535.00
1911D	515.00	535.00

1909 20 Dollar Saint Gaudens Gold Piece with Motto

Saint-Gaudens/ With Motto	VF	EF
1911S	515.00	535.00
1912	515.00	535.00
1913	515.00	535.00
1913D	515.00	535.00
1913S	550.00	800.00
1914	515.00	535.00
1914D	515.00	535.00
1914S	515.00	535.00
1915	515.00	535.00
1915S	515.00	535.00
1916S	515.00	535.00
1920	515.00	535.00
1920S	5,500.00	9,950.00
1921	8,000.00	15,000.00
1922	515.00	535.00
1922S	515.00	750.00
1923	515.00	535.00
1923D	515.00	535.00
1924	515.00	535.00

Saint-Gaudens/ With Motto	VF	EF
1924D	800.00	1,325.00
1924S	750.00	1,300.00
1925	515.00	535.00
1925D	1,000.00	1,800.00
1925S	900.00	1,350.00
1926	515.00	535.00
1926D	1,100.00	2,900.00
1926S	700.00	1,300.00
1927	515.00	535.00
1927D	—	195,000.00
1927S	2,500.00	5,000.00
1928	515.00	535.00
1929	4,750.00	7,000.00
1930S	6,000.00	15,000.00
1931	4,850.00	9,000.00
1931D	5,500.00	9,000.00
1932	7,000.00	10,000.00
1933	MS-65	7,590,000.00

U.S. PROOF SETS

Proof coins have their origins centuries ago when special carefully produced strikings were prepared as examples of the "ideal" coin, very often for reference or for royal approval. American proof coins are known at least from the early 1800s, but those proofs were not widely available. They were struck for VIPs and for those special collectors and coin dealers with personal connections at the mint.

As the proof coin developed through the late 19th and early 20th centuries, certain criteria began to characterize their manufacture. Generally these days, they are struck twice with highly polished dies on carefully prepared polished blanks. Early in the 20th century, the dies were given a matte or sandblast finish, but this soon fell out of favor. Recently, some proofs have been struck with a combination of finishes: a dull matte finish on the motifs such as portraits, with a highly reflective, mirror-like surface in the fields. These are called cameo proofs and are more desirable than conventional proofs with a mirror-like finish over the entire surface.

Beginning in 1936, the mint began the active sale of proof sets to the general public. Each set usually contains one coin of each circulating denomination. They have been released every year since with the exceptions of 1943-1949 and 1965-1967. Proof sets of the 1950s were originally sold in cardboard boxes, later in flat cellophane sheets inside a special envelope. Today they come in hard plastic cases. Proof sets not in their original holders are usually traded at a discount. Such removal can damage their fragile surfaces by exposure to breathing and humidity. Such maltreatment can cause "carbon spots," which is what collectors call the tiny black spots.

Since the mint has begun active marketing of recent commemoratives, they have also offered special proof sets containing a commemorative dollar as well as the minor coins. These are called Prestige sets.

Another option the government has offered proof set buyers since 1992 is the traditional alloy of 90 percent silver, despite the fact that no coins for circulation are struck in that composition. Special sets are also sold containing just the statehood quarters of that year.

Known Counterfeits: Proof sets are not generally counterfeited, but regular coins can occasionally be treated by pickling to look like matte proofs.

1936	**6,750.00**
1937	**3,600.00**
1938	**2,000.00**
1939	**1,850.00**
1940	**1,550.00**

1941	**1,550.00**
1942 5 coins	**1,375.00**
1942 6 coins	**1,550.00**
1950	**700.00**
1951	**630.00**
1952	**340.00**
1953	**325.00**
1954	**190.00**
1955 box	**150.00**
1955 flat pack	**200.00**
1956	**73.50**
1957	**35.00**
1958	**90.00**
1959	**29.00**
1960	**20.00**
1960 small date cent	**56.00**
1961	**11.50**
1962	**11.50**
1963	**15.00**
1964	**12.00**

1968S	**8.00**
1968S no mint mark dime	**11,000.00**
1969S	**8.00**
1970S large date cent	**16.00**
1970S small date cent	**115.00**
1970S no mint mark dime	**1,750.00**
1971S	**7.00**
1971S no mint mark nickel	**1,450.00**
1972S	**5.50**
1973S	**13.00**
1974S	**11.50**
1975S	**15.50**
1975S no mint mark dime	**50,000.00**
1976S	**9.00**
1976S 3-pc. silver	**18.50**
1977S	**8.50**
1978S	**10.00**
1979S filled S	**11.00**
1979S clear S	**130.00**
1980S	**10.00**

1981S	**10.00**
1982S	**5.50**
1983S	**7.00**
1983S no mint mark dime	**1,350.00**
1983S Prestige	**110.00**
1984S	**11.00**
1984S Prestige	**24.00**
1985S	**6.00**
1986S	**20.50**
1986S Prestige	**32.50**
1987S	**5.50**
1987S Prestige	**22.00**
1988S	**11.00**
1988S Prestige	**32.00**
1989S	**10.00**
1989S Prestige	**41.00**
1990S	**10.00**
1990S no mint mark cent	**8,000.00**
1990S Prestige	**32.00**
1990S Prestige, no mint mark cent	**8,000.00**

1995S Prestige Set

1991S	**17.50**
1991S Prestige	**80.00**
1992S	**8.50**
1992S Prestige	**160.00**
1992S Silver	**17.50**
1992S Silver Premier	**17.50**
1993S	**16.00**
1993S Prestige	**52.00**

1993S Silver	**40.00**
1993S Silver Premier	**40.00**
1994S	**25.00**
1994S Prestige	**60.00**
1994S Silver	**44.00**
1994S Silver Premier	**50.00**
1995S	**92.00**
1995S Prestige	**300.00**
1995S Silver	**108.00**
1995S Silver Premier	**110.00**
1996S	**18.00**
1996S Prestige	**500.00**
1996S Silver	**52.50**
1996S Silver Premier	**56.00**
1997S	**65.00**
1997S Prestige	**250.00**
1997S Silver	**98.00**
1997S Silver Premier	**100.00**
1998S	**38.50**
1998S Silver	**43.00**

1999 Proof Sets

1998 Silver Premier	**42.50**
1999S	**92.50**
1999S Silver	**285.00**
1999 quarters	**52.50**
2000S	**21.00**
2000S Silver	**36.00**
2000S quarters	**16.50**
2001S	**82.50**
2001S Silver	**140.00**
2001S quarters	**35.50**
2002S	**55.00**
2002S Silver	**83.50**
2002S quarters	**25.00**
2003S	**28.50**
2003S Silver	**40.00**
2003S quarters	**17.50**
2004S	—
2004S Silver	—
2004S quarters	—
2004S Silver quarters	**45.00**

U.S. MINT SETS

Mint sets do not necessarily contain coins superior to those placed in circulation. They are sold as a convenience to collectors who wish to obtain one example of each coin struck for circulation from each mint used to strike that denomination.

Mint sets from 1947 to 1958 contain two of each coin. No conventional mint sets were packaged from 1965 to 1967. The Special Mint Sets of these years were of a superior quality (despite initial government claims to the contrary) perhaps to compensate the public for the lack of proof sets available in those years.

While Philadelphia, Denver, and San Francisco were all striking coins for circulation, no mint marks were used, so their products cannot be told apart. Sets made in 1966 and 1967 came in rigid cases within a tight-fitting cardboard box. When the use of mint marks was resumed in 1968, the coins of the different mints were separated by placing them in blue or red plastic sleeves. Some recent mint sets also contain commemoratives. In 1982 and 1983, souvenir sets sold at the mint replaced mint sets.

Even more than with proof sets, mint sets must be in their original packaging to command a premium above loose, uncirculated coins. Removing them from their protective packaging can damage mint-state coins by exposure to breathing and humidity. Such maltreatment can cause "carbon spots" to form, much as they do on proof coins.

Known Counterfeits: When mint sets are presented in unofficial holders, be careful that a slightly circulated coin is not inserted in hopes of passing it off among the others. Coins that originally constituted a mint set and have been simply placed in another holder will usually have matching toning typical of early sets. The plastic holders of 1966 and 1967 can easily be opened and other coins substituted.

1947	1,300.00
1948	600.00
1949	900.00
1950	none released
1951	800.00
1952	750.00
1953	550.00
1954	290.00
1955	170.00
1956	165.00
1957	250.00
1958	160.00
1959	50.00

1960	**27.50**
1961	**45.00**
1962	**19.50**
1963	**15.00**
1964	**11.50**
1965 Special Mint Set	**12.50**
1966 Special Mint Set	**14.00**
1967 Special Mint Set	**21.00**
1968	**5.00**
1969	**7.00**
1970	**22.00**
1970 small date cent	**52.50**
1971	**4.00**
1972	**4.00**
1973	**24.00**
1974	**8.00**
1975	**11.00**
1976	**10.00**
1976S 3-pc. silver	**17.00**
1977	**8.50**

1961 Mint Set

1978	**10.00**
1979	**7.00**

This set is incomplete in that
it lacks the Susan B. Anthony
dollar.

1980	**7.00**
1981	**15.00**
1982	**Souvenir Sets only**
1983	**Souvenir Sets only**
1984	**6.00**
1985	**8.00**
1986	**22.00**
1987	**8.00**
1988	**8.00**
1989	**7.00**
1990	**7.00**
1991	**12.00**
1992	**7.00**
1993	**11.50**
1994	**11.50**
1995	**27.00**

2000D Mint Set

1996	**22.00**
1997	**23.00**
1998	**17.00**
1999	**35.00**
2000	**15.50**
2001	**23.00**
2002	**17.00**
2003	**30.00**
2004	—

2002 1 oz. Silver Walking Liberty Dollar

PAPER MONEY INTRODUCTION

Before the Civil War, there was no such thing as U.S. government paper money. During the Revolutionary War, the states and the Continental Congress printed so much paper money to finance their expenses that its value evaporated, and it became nearly worthless. As a result, when the Constitution was written it contained the words "No state shall... make anything but gold and silver coin a tender in payment of debts. (1§10)." Consequently, the government avoided issuing paper money until the Civil War, and even then it was issued under limited circumstances. The first type of paper money, Demand Notes, even bore interest.

Most of the paper money issued by the United States over the following century was redeemable for gold or silver. There are many different kinds of American paper money, as the following sections will show. Their names, usually found at the top of the note as a heading, and often the colors of their seals indicate the law that authorized their issue and the nature of their backing.

Almost all U.S. paper currency bears a date, but this is not necessarily the year it was actually printed. It is the year of the act authorizing the series or the year the series went into production. The signature combinations on banknotes can often be used to date them.

Large Size 1 Dollar Silver Certificate, Series 1899

Originally, paper money was larger than today. Until 1928, notes were about 7-1/2" by 3-1/8". Beginning with the series of 1928 (released 1929), they have been 6-1/8" x 2-5/8". The fractional notes of the Civil War were smaller than current notes, but varied in size.

GRADING PAPER MONEY

State of preservation is as important for paper money as it is for coins. Paper money is primarily graded to describe the amount of wear. Other factors can influence value though. Many of the terms used to describe the grades of paper money are the same as for coins. Of course the physical nature of paper requires a whole different set of definitions. They are briefly described here.

Crisp Uncirculated (CU)—This note is as pristine as when issued. It is literally crisp, with sharply pointed corners. It must have absolutely no folds, tears, or edge rounding. It can have no stains or staple holes either.

Extremely Fine (XF)—This is a particularly nice note with only the slightest sign of wear. It will still be crisp to the touch. Slight rounding of the corner points is possible, but no significant folds or creases. No tears, stains or staple holes at all.

A convenient method of detecting creases in a note is to hold it pointed at a narrow light source and look at it from an acute angle, though not directly in the direction of the light.

Very Fine (VF)—This is a nice clean note with obvious, but moderate, signs of wear. Creases that break the ink will be visible, but generally only one in each direction, and neither crease too deep. Its corner points will be dull. While not limp, it will have only some of the crispness of better grade notes. No significant stains will be visible.

Fine (F)—This is a worn, but not worn-out note. It has no crispness left. It will have heavy creases, but none that threaten the structural integrity of the note. Its edges may not be perfectly smooth, but are not irregularly worn. Trivial ink marks and smudges are acceptable.

Very Good (VG)—This note is worn and limp. It has serious deep creases. The edges are worn and not even. Some ink marks or smudges are visible. Tiny tears may be present, but no parts missing. Small staple or pin holes are acceptable.

Good (G)—This condition is not considered collectible for most purposes. Only the rarest of notes in this grade could find a home with most collectors. It is usually limp, heavily creased, stained, ripped, and pinned or stapled. Some of the creases will permit spots of light to shine through the note at their intersections.

HANDLING PAPER MONEY

The most important thing to know about handling currency is to *never fold paper money.* This instantaneously reduces its value. When in doubt as to whether a note has value or not, place it flat in a book until you can consult a numismatist or coin dealer. Do not carry an interesting note in your wallet. When handling a note, remember that its most fragile parts are its corners. Never touch them. Also, never repair a tear in a note with tape. The tape usually is a greater detriment to the note's value than the tear. Attempts to clean a note are also likely to cause damage.

COUNTERFEIT PAPER MONEY

Detecting counterfeit notes is not as difficult or as mysterious a business as many presume. Also, many of the methods used by merchants are so inefficiently used as to be of no value.

First, it must be realized that almost since its beginning, U.S. paper money has been printed not on paper, but on cloth. It is part cotton and part linen with some silk. The silk is in the form of minute red and blue threads which dive in and out of the surface of the note. A color copier may be able to reproduce the colors of these tiny threads, but it cannot reproduce the texture of them entering and leaving the surface of the note. Use a magnifying glass. Another key to detecting counterfeits is examining the crispness of the ink in the design. Images and lines should be sharp and distinct.

Minimal effort looking for these clues can catch most circulating counterfeits. Most counterfeit bills passed in circulation are accepted not because the counterfeits are deceptive, but because little or no effort at all is made to determine if they are genuine. This is entertainingly illustrated by the occasional news story about the cashier who accepts a spoof note in payment.

In recent years, Federal Reserve Notes have incorporated many new counterfeit detection devices to defeat high-tech reproductions. Occasionally, however, real notes have been used to create counterfeits. A counterfeiter will take the value numbers from the corners of a note and glue them to a note of a lower face value. Such notes will often feel too thick or irregular at the corners. More importantly, such a criminal is presuming the recipients will pay virtually no attention to the notes they are accepting. Such counterfeits can be detected by even the quickest comparison with a real note.

Certain practices are designed to take an authentic note and make it appear to be in a better grade of preservation than it is. These include ironing a note to make it look less worn, and expertly gluing tears. Hold your note up to a light. Light will pass through the glue differently than through normal currency.

When choosing a rare currency dealer, it is good to make sure that they have the skills to know a note is real, and the ethics to accept it back if it is not. Of course the same principles apply as mentioned above in choosing a coin dealer.

In addition to the organizations mentioned above, there are specialized organizations that also enforce codes of ethics. Two of the largest are the *International Bank Note Society* (IBNS) and the *Professional Currency Dealers Association* (PCDA). These insignia in advertising indicate that the dealer is a member.

DEMAND NOTES

The demand notes of 1861 were the very first regular paper money issued by the United States. They were put into circulation under the emergency circumstances of the Civil War. The bad experiences of the overproduction of paper money during the Revolutionary War were still remembered, so limits were set on the uses of these notes. They differed from modern currency mostly in that they were not properly legal tender, but rather were "receivable in payment for all public dues." That is to say they were not good for "all debts public and private," and not by initial obligation for any private debts at all. One could use them to pay taxes, but they did not have to be accepted otherwise. Later a law was passed requiring their acceptance. Their name Demand Note derives from another phrase on their face, "The United States promises to pay to the bearer on *demand*."

On the other hand, there were limits as to how they

could be redeemed. These notes were issued at five cities and could only be redeemed by the Assistant Treasurers in the individual note's specific city of issue. Designs were uniform from city to city. The $5 note shows at left the statue of Columbia from the Capitol building, and at right, a portrait of Alexander Hamilton. The $10 shows Lincoln, then in office, left, an eagle centered, and an allegorical figure of Art right. The $20 depicts Liberty holding a sword and shield.

The nickname "green back" for paper money began with these notes, which have a distinctive green back. The privately issued paper money circulating until then had blank backs.

There are two major varieties of demand notes, resulting from the government being ill prepared for the practical reality of hand signing millions of notes. The original intent was that clerks would be able to sign them "N. for the" Register of the Treasury and "N. for the" Treasurer of the United States. The time it took to sign the words "for the" millions of times quickly became excessive, so the notes were modified so the words were printed on instead. The earlier varieties are worth more than the prices listed here.

High-grade notes in this series are very rare.

Known Counterfeits: Examine detail, check to make sure notes are hand signed, and use reasonable caution.

Philadelphia 5 Dollar Demand Note, Series 1861

	G	VG
$5 Boston	450.00	3,500.00
$5 Cincinnati	—	rare
$5 New York	450.00	3,500.00
$5 Philadelphia	450.00	3,500.00
$5 St. Louis	1,000.00	1,500.00
$10 Boston	700.00	2,200.00
$10 Cincinnati	—	rare

	G	VG
$10 New York	700.00	2,200.00
$10 Philadelphia	700.00	2,200.00
$10 St. Louis	2,500.00	6,500.00
$20 Boston	5,500.00	13,500.00
$20 Cincinnati	—	rare
$20 New York	5,500.00	13,500.00
$20 Philadelphia	5,500.00	13,500.00

TREASURY NOTES

These notes, designated "Treasury Notes" by the titles on their face inscriptions, are also called "Coin Notes." This was because, according to law, the Secretary of the Treasury was instructed to redeem these notes in coin, either gold or silver, at his choosing. Interestingly, they were not actually backed by coin at all, but rather by silver bullion.

This series was of very short duration, being issued only in 1890 and 1891. Both years have the same face designs, generally of military heroes. The original reverse designs featured the values spelled out in large letters. For 1891, they were redesigned to allow more blank space. The ornamentation of the two 0s in 100 on the reverse of the $100 notes is reminiscent of the pattern on the skin of a watermelon, hence they are known by the collecting community as "watermelon notes."

Known Counterfeits: Examine detail, silk threads in paper, and use reasonable caution.

	F	XF
$1 1890 Edwin M. Stanton	500.00	1,300.00
$1 1891 same	250.00	450.00
$2 1890 Gen. James D. McPherson	780.00	3,200.00

2 Dollar Treasury Note, Series 1890

	F	XF
$2 1891 same	400.00	950.00
$5 1890 Gen. George H. Thomas	500.00	2,400.00
$5 1891 same	350.00	750.00
$10 1890 Gen. Philip H. Sheridan	900.00	2,500.00
$10 1891 same	550.00	1,300.00
$20 1890 John Marshall	3,350.00	7,350.00
$20 1891 same	3,300.00	7,500.00

10 Dollar Treasury Note, Series 1890

	F	XF
$50 1891 William H. Seward	22,000.00	50,000.00
$100 1890 Adm. David G. Farragut	50,000.00	100,000.00
$100 1891 same	50,000.00	100,000.00
$1000 1890 Gen. George Meade	—	rare
$1000 1891 same	—	rare

NATIONAL BANK NOTES

National bank notes are a hybrid of government issued and private paper money. The notes, titled "National Currency" on their face, were issued by individual private banks, but printed by the U.S. government. Not every bank could issue them, only "national banks." To qualify, each bank had to meet certain criteria, which included keeping a predetermined value of U.S. government bonds on deposit with the United States Treasurer. In exchange for this commitment, the notes issued by any bank were considered legal tender of the United States and were good anywhere U.S. currency was good. The Treasury would stand behind these notes.

Designs did not vary from bank to bank, but used those types designated by the Treasury. The face of each note indicated the issuing bank's name (usually including the word "national") and its charter number. Many earlier notes also showed the coat of arms of its native state.

Each of over 1,300 issuing banks was assigned a charter number. There were three periods under which banks could apply for a 20-year charter. The first period was 1863-1882. Those banks securing their charters during this period could issue notes of the first charter reverse design as late as 1902.

Banks receiving their charters from 1882 to 1902, the second period, issued notes of a new-type back designed for second-charter banks. These were actually printed 1882 to 1922.

Those banks receiving their charters during the third period of authorization, 1902 to 1922, issued yet a third series of different designs from 1902 to 1929. It is seen that this system determines the design (and often apparent "date") on a note not by when it was issued, but by when the issuing bank first received its charter. Hence, different designs of a National Bank Note could be issued at the same time with different dates! A very confusing situation.

Like all other currency, Nationals were reduced in size in 1929. Type 1 notes (1929-33) have the charter number on the face twice. Type 2 notes (1933-35) have it four times. In May 1935, when the Treasury recalled many of the bonds that the national banks were using as security, National Bank Notes ceased to be issued.

Nationals have been among the most sought-after notes in a generally active U.S. paper money market. Not all nationals of a given type are worth the same, as certain states and cities are more popularly collected than others. Also, some banks ordered very small quantities of notes. The values below are for the most common and least expensive banks issuing that type of note. Large-size nationals from Alaska, Arizona,

Hawaii, Idaho, Indian Territory, Mississippi, Nevada, New Mexico, Puerto Rico, and South Dakota are automatically worth more. The same is true for small-size nationals from Alaska, Arizona, Hawaii, Idaho, Montana, Nevada, and Wyoming.

Known Counterfeits: Examine detail, silk threads in paper, and use reasonable caution.

First Charter (1863-1875)	VG	VF
$1 Allegory of Concord/ Pilgrims landing, ND (original series)	700.00	1,100.00
same, 1875	700.00	1,100.00
$2 Lazy 2/Sir Walter Raleigh, ND (Original series)	2,900.00	4,300.00
same, 1875	2,900.00	4,300.00
$5 Columbus sighting land/ landing of Columbus, ND (original series)	990.00	1,700.00
same, 1875	990.00	1,700.00
$10 Franklin experimenting with lightning/DeSoto, ND (original series)	1,200.00	2,100.00
same, 1875	1,200.00	2,100.00

First Charter (1863-1875)	VG	VF
$20 Battle of Lexington/ baptism of Pocahontas, ND (original series)	1,800.00	2,750.00
same, 1875	1,800.00	2,750.00
$50 Washington Crossing Delaware and at prayer/ Pilgrims, ND (original series)	8,500.00	15,000.00
$100 Battle of Lake Erie/ signing of the Declaration of Independence, ND (original series)	9,900.00	18,500.00
$500	—	unique
$1000	—	unique

Second Charter/Series of 1882 "Brown Backs" with charter number	VG	VF
$5 James Garfield	550.00	750.00
$10 as 1st charter	700.00	1,100.00
$20 as 1st charter	885.00	1,300.00
$50 as 1st charter	3,400.00	4,700.00
$100 as 1st charter	5,500.00	7,000.00

50 Dollar National Bank Note, Third Charter

Second Charter/Series of 1882 "Date Backs" with large "1882*1908"	VG	VF
$5 James Garfield	550.00	750.00
$10 as 1st charter	700.00	1,100.00
$20 as 1st charter	885.00	1,300.00
$50 as 1st charter	3,400.00	4,700.00
$100 as 1st charter	5,500.00	7,000.00

Second Charter/Series of 1882 "Value Backs" large spelled-out value	VG	VF
$5 James Garfield	550.00	750.00
$10 as 1st charter	700.00	1,100.00
$20 as 1st charter	885.00	1,300.00
$50 as 1st charter	36,000.00	50,000.00
$100 as 2nd series	85,000.00	extremely rare

Third Charter/Series of 1902 Red Treasury Seal on face	VG	VF
$5 Benjamin Harrison/Pilgrims landing	550.00	750.00
$10 William McKinley/ Columbia between ships	700.00	1,100.00
$20 Hugh McCulloch/Columbia and Capitol	885.00	1,300.00
$50 John Sherman/train	3,400.00	4,700.00
$100 John Knox/eagle on shield	5,500.00	7,000.00

Third Charter/Series of 1902 Blue Treasury Seal, "1902-1908" on back	VG	VF
$5 as red seals	200.00	300.00
$10 as red seals	200.00	300.00
$20 as red seals	200.00	300.00
$50 as red seals	1,300.00	1,800.00
$100 as red seals	1,800.00	2,500.00

*5 Dollar Small Size, Type 2 National Bank Note
(serial number and bank number in brown), Series 1929*

Third Charter/Series of 1902 Blue Treasury Seal, "Plain Backs" without dates	VG	VF
$5 as red seals	200.00	300.00
$10 as red seals	200.00	300.00
$20 as red seals	200.00	
$50 as red seals	1,300.00	1,800.00
$100 as red seals	1,800.00	2,500.00

50 Dollar Small Size National Bank Note, Type 2, Series 1929

Third Charter/Series of 1929 Brown Treasury Seal, Small-Size Notes	VG	VF
$5 Type 1	100.00	120.00
$5 Type 2	100.00	120.00
$10 Type 1	100.00	120.00
$10 Type 2	100.00	120.00
$20 Type 1	110.00	120.00
$20 Type 2	110.00	120.00
$50 Type 1	340.00	380.00
$50 Type 2	340.00	380.00
$100 Type 1	480.00	550.00
$100 Type 2	480.00	600.00

NATIONAL GOLD BANK NOTES

These notes were like National Bank Notes, but they were specifically redeemable in gold coin. They were a co-operative issue of the individual National Gold Bank that held the obligation, and the U.S. Treasury. Every bank had to be a regular national bank as well and meet all the reserve requirements. But these national banks were authorized by the Treasury to issue notes redeemable in gold.

The reason for their issue from 1870-75 was to relieve the banks in California of the daily handling of massive quantities of gold coin. All but one of the banks authorized to issue these was located in California. The very design of these notes reflects their backing by gold. Their paper is a golden yellow, and the reverse bears an array of United States gold coins of every denomination. Their remarkably fine engraving gives the coins a very realistic appearance. Because other types of notes were not very popular in California, these notes got some very hard use, and today are rare in all but worn-out condition.

Known Counterfeits: Examine detail, and look for correct yellow paper, which occasionally may tone down. Use reasonable caution.

	G	F
$5 Columbus sighting land	950.00	2,400.00
$10 Franklin experimenting with lightning	2,500.00	4,800.00
$20 Battle of Lexington	4,000.00	10,000.00
$50 Washington crossing Delaware and at prayer	15,000.00	rare
$100 Battle of Lake Erie	38,000.00	rare

UNITED STATES NOTES

While most of these notes carry the title "United States Note" at the top or bottom of their face, some earlier ones actually say "Treasury Note" instead. The very first notes omit both. They are, however, the same according to the legislation that authorized them. They are the longest-lasting kind of American paper money, being issued for over a century, from 1862 until 1966. There are a great many different designs, of which the "Bison Ten" is the most famous and most popular.

Like all other currency, United States Notes were reduced in size with the "series of 1928" in 1929. Small-size notes are occasionally found in circulation today, and are characterized by a red Treasury seal. The latter, when worn, are not generally considered collectible.

This series includes popular "star" notes. These are notes with part of the serial number replaced by a star. They were printed to replace notes accidentally destroyed in manufacturing. These were introduced first on $20 notes in 1880 and eventually descended to $1 notes by 1917. They usually are worth more.

Known Counterfeits: Examine detail, silk threads in paper, and use reasonable caution. In addition to counterfeits made to fool collectors, early circulation counterfeits of the 1863 $50, 1869 $50, and 1863 $100 exist.

Large Size	F	XF
$1 1862 Salmon P. Chase, red seal	400.00	800.00
$1 1869 Washington, Columbus scene/US intertwined	400.00	900.00
$1 1874-1917 same/large X	85.00	95.00
$1 1923 Washington bust	95.00	150.00
$2 1862 Alexander Hamilton double circle	600.00	1,600.00
$2 1869 Jefferson and Capitol/ II•2•TWO	600.00	1,600.00
$2 1874-1917 same/II•TWO omitted	90.00	150.00
$5 1862 Statue of Columbia l., Alexander Hamilton r.	445.00	830.00
$5 1863 same, different obligation on back	445.00	830.00
$5 1869 Jackson l., pioneer family center/circle with 5	400.00	840.00
$5 1875-1907 same, red seal/ circle with concentric pattern	110.00	230.00
$5 1880 same, brown seal	195.00	540.00

2 Dollar Large Size United States Note, Series 1875

Large Size	F	VF
$10 1862 Lincoln and allegory of Art	850.00	2,200.00
$10 1862-63 same, different obligation on back	850.00	2,200.00
$10 1869 Daniel Webster and Pocahontas/inscription centered	600.00	1,300.00

5 Dollar Large Size United States Note, Series 1869

Large Size	F	VF
$10 1875-80 same/inscription at right	390.00	780.00
$10 1880 same, brown seal	435.00	940.00
$10 1901 Bison/Columbia standing between pillars	560.00	1,200.00
$10 1923 Andrew Jackson/value	800.00	1,800.00

10 Dollar Large Size United States Note, Series 1862

Large Size	F	VF
$20 1862 Liberty with sword and shield	1,900.00	4,200.00
$20 1862-63 same, different obligation on back	1,900.00	4,200.00
$20 1869 Alexander Hamilton l., Victory standing r.	1,950.00	3,600.00
$20 1875-80 same/no inscription at center	400.00	900.00

10 Dollar Large Size United States Note, Series 1901

Large Size	F	VF
$20 1880 same, brown seal	1,200.00	3,000.00
$50 1862 Alexander Hamilton	9,000.00	22,500.00
$50 1862-63 same, different obligation on back	8,250.00	22,000.00
$50 1869 Peace and Henry Clay	14,500.00	40,000.00
$50 1874-80 Franklin and Columbia	2,800.00	6,000.00

Large Size	F	VF
$50 same, brown seal	4,100.00	7,100.00
$100 1862 Eagle	15,000.00	34,000.00
$100 1862-63 same, different obligation on back	15,000.00	34,000.00
$100 1869 Lincoln and allegory of Architecture/inscription centered	14,500.00	30,000.00
$100 1875-80 same, inscription at left	4,500.00	15,000.00
$100 1880, same, brown seal	6,000.00	20,000.00
$500 1862 Albert Gallatin	—	rare
$500 1862-63 same, different obligation on back	—	rare
$500 1869 John Quincy Adams	—	rare
$500 1874-80 Gen. Joseph Mansfield	—	rare
$500 1880 same, brown seal	—	rare
$1000 1862 Robert Morris	—	rare
$1000 1862-63 same, different obligation on back	—	rare

Large Size	F	VF
$1000 1869 Columbus and DeWitt Clinton/inscription centered	—	rare
$1000 1878-80 same, inscription at left	—	rare
$1000 1880 same, brown seal	—	rare

Small Size U.S. Notes—Red Seal

Denom.	Issue	Front	Back
$1	1928	Washington	ONE
$2	1928-63A	Jefferson	Monticello
$5	1928-63	Lincoln	Lincoln Memorial
$100	1966-66A	Franklin	Indep. Hall

Small Size—Red Seal	F	XF
$1 1928	55.00	130.00
$2 1928	13.50	25.00
$2 1928A	45.00	95.00
$2 1928B	60.00	255.00
$2 1928C	13.00	27.00
$2 1928D	10.00	16.00
$2 1928E	15.00	30.00
$2 1928F	5.00	18.00
$2 1928G	5.00	15.00

1 Dollar Small Size United States Note, Red Seal, Series 1928

Small Size—Red Seal	CU
$2 1953	10.00
$2 1953A	10.00
$2 1953B	10.00
$2 1953C	10.00
$2 1963	8.00

5 Dollar Small Size United States Note, Red Seal, Series 1928

Small Size—Red Seal	F	XF
$2 1963A		10.00
$5 1928	12.00	30.00
$5 1928A	15.00	40.00
$5 1928B	12.00	25.00
$5 1928C	12.00	25.00
$5 1928D	30.00	75.00

Small Size—Red Seal	F	XF
$5 1928E	10.00	20.00
$5 1928F	10.00	20.00
$5 1953	8.50	15.00
$5 1953A	7.00	12.00
$5 1953B	7.00	12.00
$5 1953C	7.50	15.00
$5 1963	7.00	12.00
$100 1966	200.00	400.00
$100 1966A	350.00	1,000.00

GOLD CERTIFICATES

As the title on these notes implies, these were notes both backed by reserves in gold coin and payable to the bearer in that coin. The first Gold Certificates were issued in 1865-75, but were used for transactions between banks. Notes of this period not listed following are not known to have survived. The issue of 1882 was the first for general circulation. The issues of 1888-89 were only of $5,000 and $10,000 and not widely circulated.

Regular issues were again placed in circulation in 1905-07. This series includes a $20 note so beautifully colored with black, red and gold ink on white gold-tinted paper that it has acquired the nickname

"Technicolor." Those of the series of 1913-28 are the most common Gold Certificates.

Like all other notes of the 1928 series, these gold certificates were printed on the reduced-size paper still used today. These are distinguished from other kinds of small-size notes by a gold Treasury seal. The final issues, those of 1934, were again just for bank transactions. The government recalled these notes from general circulation in 1933 when it withdrew gold coinage. Today, they are perfectly legal to own but far scarcer due to this earlier destruction.

Known Counterfeits: Examine detail on 1882 and later silk threads in paper, and use reasonable caution.

First Issue—1863	F	XF
$20 Eagle on shield	—	extremely rare
$100 Eagle on shield	—	extremely rare

Second Issue—1870-71
No notes known to have survived.

Third Issue—1870s		
$100 Thomas H. Benton	—	extremely rare

Fourth Issue—Series of 1882	F	XF
$20 James Garfield	3,500.00	10,000.00
$50 Silas Wright	1,250.00	3,500.00
$100 Thomas Benton	900.00	2,500.00
$500 Abraham Lincoln	7,000.00	25,000.00
$1000 Alexander Hamilton	—	rare
$5000 James Madison	—	rare
$10,000 Andrew Jackson	—	rare
Fifth Issue—Series of 1888		
$5000 James Madison	—	rare
$10,000 Andrew Jackson	—	rare
Sixth Issue—Series of 1900		
$10,000 Jackson	cut cancelled	1,400.00
Seventh Issue—Series of 1905-07		
$10 Michael Hillegas	150.00	340.00
$20 Washington 1905 "technicolor note"	1,250.00	3,800.00
$20 Washington 1906	230.00	535.00

Eighth Issue—Series of 1907	F	XF
$1000 Alexander Hamilton	10,000.00	rare

Ninth Issue—Series of 1913	F	XF
$50 Ulysses S. Grant	720.00	1,350.00

Tenth Issue—Series of 1922	F	XF
$10 Michael Hillegas	150.00	330.00
$20 Washington	250.00	450.00
$50 Ulysses S. Grant	650.00	1,250.00
$100 Thomas Benton	650.00	1,700.00
$500 Abraham Lincoln	—	rare
$1000 Alexander Hamilton	—	rare

Small Size—Series of 1928	F	XF
$10 Alex. Hamilton	70.00	125.00
$20 Andrew Jackson	95.00	150.00
$50 Ulysses S. Grant	400.00	650.00
$100 Ben. Franklin	500.00	850.00
$500 W. McKinley	2,500.00	8,000.00
$1000 G. Cleveland	2,800.00	9,000.00
$5000 James Madison	—	rare

10 Dollar Small Size Gold Certificate, Series 1928

SILVER CERTIFICATES

On February 28, 1878, the same day that Congress authorized the striking of millions of silver dollars, it also passed legislation authorizing Silver Certificates. This is not pure coincidence. Silver Certificates were not simply backed up by silver bullion, but represented actual silver dollars held by the Treasury. The issue of this series of notes was what in part made it necessary to strike millions of Morgan dollars, and was ultimately prompted by heavy lobbying by the silver mining industry.

Some of the most famous and beautiful banknotes issued by the U.S. are Silver Certificates. These include the "Educational" $1, $2, and $5 of 1896, the "Onepapa Five," and the "Porthole Five." The name "Onepapa Five" is a misnomer. It depicts Chief Running Antelope of the Uncpapa Sioux, but because the name sounded so unfamiliar to early collectors it was quickly mispronounced "Chief One Papa."

Like all other currency, Silver Certificates were reduced in size with the "series of 1928" in 1929.

During World War II, there was fear that supplies of U.S. currency would fall into enemy hands if certain territories were overrun. The response to this was to make sure that notes distributed in these territories had distinguishing features that permitted their identification and repudiation if captured. Silver Certificates issued to troops in North Africa were printed with a yellow Treasury seal instead of a blue one. Notes distributed in Hawaii feature the word HAWAII overprinted very large on the back.

The motto "In God We Trust" was added to the one-dollar note for the 1935G and H and all 1957 series. They continued to be issued until the 1957B series in 1963. Small-size silver certificates are occasionally found in circulation today and are easily recognized by a blue Treasury seal. These notes when worn are generally not considered collectible, but do have some novelty value. They have not been redeemable for silver dollars since 1968.

This series includes popular "star" notes. These are notes with part of the serial number replaced by a star. They are printed to replace notes accidentally destroyed in the manufacturing process. These were introduced first in 1899. They often, but not always, are worth somewhat more.

Known Counterfeits: Examine detail, silk threads in paper, and use reasonable caution. Circulating counterfeits exist for this series and are slightly less dangerous.

Large Size	F	XF
$1 1886 Martha Washington/ inscription in oval	275.00	700.00
$1 1891 same/inscription in rosette	300.00	650.00
$1 1896 History instructing youth/George and Martha Washington	340.00	630.00
$1 1899 Eagle	85.00	160.00
$1 1923 Washington	40.00	50.00
$2 1886 Gen. Winfield Scott Hancock	580.00	1,270.00

1 Dollar Large Size Silver Certificate, Series 1896

Large Size	F	XF
$2 1891 Sen. William Windom	465.00	1,350.00
$2 1896 Science Presenting Steam and Electricity to Commerce and Industry/Fulton and Morse	560.00	1,800.00
$2 1899 Washington, Mechanics and Agriculture	250.00	435.00

2 Dollar Large Size Silver Certificate, Series 1896

Large Size	F	XF
$5 1886 Ulysses S. Grant/ Morgan silver dollars	730.00	2,500.00
$5 1891 same/inscription	510.00	1,375.00
$5 1896 Winged Electricity lighting the World	1,000.00	2,850.00

5 Dollar Large Size Silver Certificate, Series 1899

Large Size	F	XF
$5 1899 Chief "Onepapa"	480.00	995.00
$5 1923 Lincoln in porthole-like frame/great seal	500.00	1,200.00
$10 1878-80 Robert Morris/ S I L V E R	1,450.00	3,600.00
$10 1886 Thomas Hendricks in tombstone-like frame	700.00	2,600.00

10 Dollar Large Size Siver Certificate, 1891 Series

Large Size	F	XF
$10 1891-1908 same/UNITED STATES in oval	410.00	1,250.00
$20 1878-80 Capt. Stephen Decatur/S I L V E R	3,500.00	10,000.00
$20 1886 Daniel Manning/ double diamond	3,300.00	7,500.00
$20 1891 same/double circle	990.00	2,300.00

Large Size	F	XF
$50 1878-80 Edward Everett/ S I L V E R	**8,000.00**	**30,000.00**
$50 1891 same/inscription in center	**2,300.00**	**4,500.00**
$100 1878-80 James Monroe/S I L V E R	**10,000.00**	**33,000.00**
$100 1891 same/inscription in center	**7,500.00**	**15,000.00**
$500 1878-80 Sen. Charles Sumner/S I L V E R	—	**rare**
$1000 1878-80 William Marcy	—	**rare**
$1000 1891 Columbia and Marcy	—	**rare**

Small Size Silver Certificates—Blue Seal

Denom.	Issue	Front	Back
$1	1928-28E	Washington	ONE
$1	1934-57B	Washington	Great Seal
$5	1934-53C	Lincoln	Lincoln Memorial
$10	1933-53B	Hamilton	Treasury

Small Size—Blue Seal	F	XF
$1 1928	**10.00**	**25.00**
$1 1928A	**10.00**	**25.00**
$1 1928B	**10.00**	**27.00**

SMALL SIZE SILVER CERTIFICATES—BLUE SEAL

Small Size—Blue Seal	F	XF
$1 1928C	140.00	3,200.00
$1 1928D	45.00	115.00
$1 1928E	325.00	650.00
$1 1934	13.00	28.00
$1 1935	5.00	9.00
$1 1935A	3.00	5.00
$1 1935A HAWAII	25.00	42.00
$1 1935A yellow seal	22.00	38.00
$1 1935A red R	45.00	100.00
$1 1935A red S	40.00	90.00
$1 1935B	2.50	4.00
$1 1935C	2.50	3.50
$1 1935D	2.00	3.00
$1 1935E	—	7.00
$1 1935F	—	7.00
$1 1935G	—	8.00
same with motto	4.00	30.00
$1 1935H	—	10.00

Small Size—Blue Seal	F	XF
$1 1957	—	5.00
$1 1957A	—	6.50
$1 1957B	—	6.50
$5 1934	10.00	34.00
$5 1934A	10.00	20.00

1 Dollar Small Size Silver Certificate, Blue Seal, Series 1928

Small Size—Blue Seal	F	XF
$5 1934A yellow seal	65.00	200.00
$5 1934B	18.00	40.00
$5 1934C	12.00	25.00
$5 1934D	10.00	20.00
$5 1953	—	20.00
$5 1953A	—	16.00

5 Dollar Small Size Silver Certificate, Special Yellow Seal, Series 1934A

Small Size—Blue Seal	F	XF
$5 1953B	—	16.00
$10 1933	6,300.00	12,500.00
$10 1933A	—	unique
$10 1934	35.00	95.00
$10 1934A	42.00	125.00
$10 1934 yellow seal	7,000.00	20,000.00

5 Dollar Small Size Silver Certificate, Blue Seal, Series 1934B

Small Size—Blue Seal	F	XF
$10 1934A yellow seal	85.00	200.00
$10 1934B	275.00	1,600.00
$10 1934C	45.00	100.00
$10 1934D	40.00	150.00

10 Dollar Small Size Silver Certificate, Blue Seal, Series 1933

Small Size—Blue Seal	F	XF
$10 1953	55.00	150.00
$10 1953A	90.00	200.00
$10 1953B	55.00	125.00

*10 Dollar Small Size Silver Certificate,
Special Yellow Seal, Series 1934A*

FEDERAL RESERVE NOTES

The Federal Reserve System was created in 1913. Under this system, there are 12 Federal Reserve Banks. They are governed in part by the U.S. government through the Federal Reserve Board, appointed by the President, and confirmed by the Senate. Each of the Federal Reserve Banks is composed of various member banks.

Today in the United States, the paper currency is not directly issued by the Treasury, but by the Federal Reserve Banks. Originally, Federal Reserve Notes bore an obligation of the government to redeem them in gold. This was changed in 1934. Today, Federal Reserve Notes are the only type of paper money issued in the United States.

Like all other currency, Federal Reserve Notes were reduced in size with the "series of 1928" in 1929.

Since 1993, major new innovations have been gradually added to these notes to prevent counterfeiting. At first, micro printing was incorporated in the design and around the frame of the portrait. Also, a transparent strip bearing the value and USA was imbedded inside the paper. It can only be seen when the note is held up to the light and cannot be photocopied.

These improvements were only a precursor to the first major overhaul of the designs of the currency since the 1920s. Beginning in 1996, with the $100 bill, additional features were added, including the enlargment of portraits to show more detail, and the modification of the reverse to add more white space, making it possible to successfully use a watermark incorporated into the paper. A watermark is an image neither printed on nor imbedded inside the paper, but one created by the pressure of a pattern pressed against the paper during its drying stage. Like the transparent printed strip, it can only be seen when the note is held up to the light.

Among the most ingenious high-tech safeguards on the new notes is the use of color shifting ink, which alters its color depending on the angle of the light hitting it. The green Treasury seal has been retained, but the old letter seal indicating the Federal Reserve Bank of distribution is now replaced by the seal of the Federal Reserve system. These innovations were also incorporated into the 1996 series $50 and $20 notes, with the $10 and $5 notes following during the 1999 series. The $1 note is intended to remain basically the same.

In 2004, additional steps were taken to prevent counterfeiting. Both the $20 and $50 note received multi-color background designs. The change is also scheduled for the $10 in 2005, and for the $100 after $10.

A recent experiment with the use of a Web Press in the manufacture of $1 notes has resulted in less than total success. Interestingly enough for collectors, however, is the fact that this has resulted in some paper

money being printed outside the Bureau of Engraving and Printing for the first time since the 19th century, and the appearance of an actual mint mark, FW being used to designate Fort Worth, Texas.

Most Federal Reserve Notes since the 1930s are only collected in high grade. Dealers may be unwilling to buy even scarce pieces if not crisp uncirculated. Star replacement notes are quite popularly collected in this series, but again, must usually be crisp to be desirable. Very recent ones command no premium at all, and are sold at face value plus a handling fee to cover the dealer's labor.

Known Counterfeits: Examine detail, silk threads in paper, and use reasonable caution. Circulating counterfeits exist, particularly $20, and to a lesser extent the $10. Most are imperfect, and can be easily detected on close examination. The $100 is the most counterfeited outside the United States.

Red Seal—Series of 1914	F	XF
$5 Abraham Lincoln/Columbus and Pilgrims	350.00	650.00
$10 Andrew Jackson/reaper and factory	330.00	750.00
$20 Grover Cleveland/train and ship	500.00	1,100.00

10 Dollar Large Size Federal
Reserve Note, Red Seal, Series 1914

Red Seal—Series of 1914	F	XF
$50 Ulysses S. Grant/allegory of Panama	1,200.00	2,250.00
$100 Franklin/five allegories including commerce and agriculture	1,500.00	3,000.00

5 Dollar Large Size Federal
Reserve Note, Blue Seal, Series 1914

Blue Seal—Series of 1914	F	XF
$5 Abraham Lincoln/Columbus and Pilgrims	55.00	90.00
$10 Andrew Jackson/Reaper and factory	65.00	110.00
$20 Grover Cleveland/train and ship	100.00	150.00

*10 Dollar Large Size Federal
Reserve Note, Blue Seal, Series 1914*

Blue Seal—Series of 1914	F	XF
$50 Ulysses S. Grant/allegory of Panama	200.00	460.00
$100 Franklin/five allegories including commerce and agriculture	525.00	700.00

*1,000 Dollar Large Size Federal
Reserve Note, Blue Seal, Series 1918*

Blue Seal—Series of 1918	F	XF
$500 John Marshall/DeSoto discovering Mississippi	5,000.00	12,000.00
$1,000 Alexander Hamilton/ eagle	6,200.00	15,000.00
$5,000 Madison	—	extremely rare
$10,000 Chase	—	extremely rare

Small Size Notes—Green Seal

Denom.	Issue	Front	Back
$1	1963	Washington	great seal
$2	1976	Jefferson	Signing Declaration
$5	1928	Lincoln	Lincoln Memorial
$10	1928	Hamilton	Treasury Building
$20	1928	Jackson	White House
$50	1928	Grant	Capitol
$100	1928	Franklin	Independence Hall
$500	1928-34A	McKinley	500
$1000	1928-34A	Cleveland	inscription
$5000	1928-34B	Madison	5000
$10,000	1928-34B	Chase	10,000

One Dollar	F	XF
$1 1963	—	3.00
$1 1963A	—	3.00
$1 1963B	—	3.50
$1 1969	—	2.50
$1 1969A	—	2.50
$1 1969B	—	2.50
$1 1969C	—	2.50
$1 1969D	—	2.50
$1 1974	—	2.00

*1 Dollar Small Size Federal
Reserve Note, Green Seal, Series 1963*

One Dollar	F	XF
$1 1977	—	2.00
$1 1977A	—	2.00
$1 1981	—	2.00
$1 1981A	—	3.00
$1 1985	—	2.00
$1 1988	—	2.50

One Dollar	F	XF
$1 1988A, DC	—	2.00
$1 1988A, FW	—	2.00
$1 1988A web press	4.00	30.00
$1 1993, DC	—	2.00
$1 1993, FW	—	2.00
$1 1993 web press	3.00	15.00
$1 1995, DC	—	2.00
$1 1995, FW	—	2.00
$1 1995 web press	3.00	15.00
$1 1999, DC	—	2.00
$1 1999, FW	—	2.00
$1 2001, DC	—	2.00
$1 2001, FW	—	2.00
$1 2003, DC	—	2.00
$1 2003, FW	—	2.00

Two Dollars	XF	CU
$2 1976	—	4.00
$2 1995	—	4.00

*5 Dollar Small Size Federal
Reserve Note, Green Seal, Series 1928A*

Five Dollars	XF	CU
$5 1928	35.00	100.00
$5 1928A	25.00	95.00
$5 1928B	25.00	50.00
$5 1928C	220.00	600.00

Five Dollars	XF	CU
$5 1928D	1,200.00	2,500.00
$5 1934	20.00	45.00
$5 1934A	20.00	30.00
$5 1934 HAWAII	100.00	450.00
$5 1934A HAWAII	125.00	450.00
$5 1934B	20.00	40.00
$5 1934C	20.00	50.00
$5 1934D	20.00	50.00
$5 1950	—	45.00
$5 1950A	—	20.00
$5 1950B	—	20.00
$5 1950C	—	15.00
$5 1950D	—	15.00
$5 1950E	—	25.00
$5 1963	—	15.00
$5 1963A	—	12.00
$5 1969	—	10.00
$5 1969A	—	12.00
$5 1969B	—	35.00

5 Dollar Small Size Federal
Reserve Note, Green Seal, Series 1950A

Five Dollars	XF	CU
$5 1969C	—	12.00
$5 1974	—	10.00
$5 1977	—	10.00
$5 1977A	—	10.00
$5 1981	—	10.00

*5 Dollar Small Size Federal
Reserve Note, Green Seal, Series 1969*

Five Dollars	XF	CU
$5 1981A	—	10.00
$5 1985	—	10.00
$5 1988	—	10.00
$5 1988A	—	10.00
$5 1993	—	10.00

10 Dollar Small Size Federal
Reserve Note, Green Seal, Series 1928

Five Dollars	XF	CU
$5 1995	—	10.00
$5 1999 large portrait	—	10.00
$5 2001	—	10.00
$5 2003	—	10.00

Ten Dollars	XF	CU
$10 1928	60.00	250.00

*10 Dollar Small Size Federal
Reserve Note, Green Seal, Series 1934*

Ten Dollars	XF	CU
$10 1928A	60.00	400.00
$10 1928B	30.00	75.00
$10 1928C	60.00	350.00
$10 1934	18.00	45.00
$10 1934A	15.00	30.00

*10 Dollar Small Size Federal
Reserve Note, Green Seal, Series 1950A*

Ten Dollars	XF	CU
$10 1934A HAWAII	125.00	500.00
$10 1934B	25.00	75.00
$10 1934C	15.00	30.00
$10 1934D	15.00	35.00
$10 1950	20.00	65.00

*10 Dollar Small Size Federal
Reserve Note, Green Seal, Series 1969*

Ten Dollars	XF	CU
$10 1950A	15.00	35.00
$10 1950B	—	30.00
$10 1950C	—	35.00
$10 1950D	—	35.00
$10 1950E	—	30.00

*10 Dollar Small Size Federal
Reserve Note, Green Seal, Series 1977*

Ten Dollars	XF	CU
$10 1963	—	35.00
$10 1963A	—	25.00
$10 1969	—	25.00
$10 1969A	—	25.00
$10 1969B	—	25.00

*10 Dollar Small Size Federal
Reserve Note, Green Seal, Series 2003*

Ten Dollars	XF	CU
$10 1969C	—	30.00
$10 1974	—	25.00
$10 1977	—	30.00
$10 1977A	—	25.00
$10 1981	—	35.00

Ten Dollars	XF	CU
$10 1981A	—	35.00
$10 1985	—	25.00
$10 1988A	—	25.00
$10 1990	—	15.00
$10 1993	—	15.00
$10 1995	—	15.00
$10 1999 large portrait	—	15.00
$10 2001	—	15.00
$10 2003	—	15.00

Twenty Dollars	XF	CU
$20 1928	75.00	175.00
$20 1928A	75.00	300.00
$20 1928B	50.00	100.00
$20 1928C	750.00	1,500.00
$20 1934	40.00	45.00
$20 1934A	40.00	60.00
$20 1934 HAWAII	200.00	800.00
$20 1934A HAWAII	100.00	650.00

*20 Dollar Small Size Federal
Reserve Note, Green Seal, Series 1928*

Twenty Dollars	XF	CU
$20 1934B	35.00	75.00
$20 1934C	40.00	75.00
$20 1934D	—	45.00
$20 1950	—	60.00
$20 1950A	—	60.00

20 Dollar Small Size Federal
Reserve Note, Green Seal, Series 1934

Twenty Dollars	XF	CU
$20 1950B	—	45.00
$20 1950C	—	60.00
$20 1950D	—	60.00
$20 1950E	—	75.00
$20 1963	—	60.00

20 Dollar Small Size Federal
Reserve Note, Green Seal, Series 1950D

Twenty Dollars	XF	CU
$20 1963A	—	**45.00**
$20 1969	—	**45.00**
$20 1969A	—	**50.00**
$20 1969B	—	**100.00**
$20 1969C	—	**45.00**

*20 Dollar Small Size Federal
Reserve Note, Green Seal, Series 1974*

Twenty Dollars	XF	CU
$20 1974	—	45.00
$20 1977	—	45.00
$20 1981	—	60.00
$20 1981A	—	45.00
$20 1985	—	40.00

Twenty Dollars	XF	CU
$20 1988A	—	45.00
$20 1990	—	30.00
$20 1993	—	30.00
$20 1995	—	30.00
$20 1996 large portrait	—	30.00
$20 1999 large portrait	—	25.00
$20 2001, DC, large portrait	—	25.00
$20 2001, FW, large portrait	—	25.00
$20 2004, large portrait, colorized background	—	25.00

Fifty Dollars	XF	CU
$50 1928	125.00	450.00
$50 1928A	90.00	300.00
$50 1934	75.00	225.00
$50 1934A	90.00	250.00
$50 1934B	125.00	300.00
$50 1934C	110.00	175.00
$50 1934D	75.00	200.00
$50 1950	70.00	200.00

*50 Dollar Small Size Federal
Reserve Note, Green Seal, Series 1928*

Fifty Dollars	XF	CU
$50 1950A	70.00	200.00
$50 1950B	60.00	120.00
$50 1950C	65.00	150.00
$50 1950D	60.00	120.00
$50 1950E	200.00	500.00

*50 Dollar Small Size Federal
Reserve Note, Green Seal, Series 1950*

Fifty Dollars	XF	CU
$50 1963A	—	100.00
$50 1969	—	150.00
$50 1969A	—	140.00
$50 1969B	—	600.00
$50 1969C	—	100.00

50 Dollar Small Size Federal
Reserve Note, Green Seal, Series 1969A

Fifty Dollars	XF	CU
$50 1974	—	100.00
$50 1977	—	80.00
$50 1981	—	125.00
$50 1981A	—	150.00
$50 1985	—	75.00

Fifty Dollars	XF	CU
$50 1988	—	95.00
$50 1990	—	65.00
$50 1993	—	65.00
$50 1996 large portrait	—	60.00
$50 2001 large portrait	—	60.00
$50 2004 large portrait, colorized background	—	60.00

One Hundred Dollars	XF	CU
$100 1928	250.00	600.00
$100 1928A	175.00	250.00
$100 1934	175.00	250.00
$100 1934A	180.00	300.00
$100 1934B	400.00	600.00
$100 1934C	175.00	400.00
$100 1934D	350.00	450.00
$100 1950	—	450.00
$100 1950A	—	200.00
$100 1950B	—	250.00
$100 1950C	—	275.00

*100 Dollar Small Size Federal
Reserve Note, Green Seal, Series 1928A*

One Hundred Dollars	XF	CU
$100 1950D	—	250.00
$100 1950E	—	600.00
$100 1963A	—	200.00
$100 1969	—	175.00
$100 1969A	—	175.00

*100 Dollar Small Size Federal
Reserve Note, Green Seal, Series 1934B*

One Hundred Dollars	XF	CU
$100 1969C	—	175.00
$100 1974	—	150.00
$100 1977	—	175.00
$100 1981	—	200.00
$100 1981A	—	200.00

*100 Dollar Small Size Federal
Reserve Note, Green Seal, Series 1963A*

One Hundred Dollars	XF	CU
$100 1985	—	150.00
$100 1988	—	150.00
$100 1990	—	125.00
$100 1993	—	120.00

One Hundred Dollars	XF	CU
$100 1996 large portrait	—	120.00
$100 1999, DC, large portrait	—	120.00
$100 1999, FW, large portrait	—	120.00
$100 2001 large portrait	—	120.00

Five Hundred Dollars	XF	CU
$500 1928	1,200.00	2,500.00
$500 1934	950.00	1,200.00
$500 1934A	950.00	1,200.00
$500 1934B	550.00	675.00
$500 1934C	550.00	650.00

One Thousand Dollars	XF	CU
$1000 1928	2,250.00	2,800.00
$1000 1934	2,000.00	2,400.00
$1000 1934A	2,000.00	2,400.00
$1000 1934C	1,250.00	1,500.00

Five Thousand Dollars	XF	CU
$5000 1928	40,000.00	60,000.00
$5000 1934	35,000.00	50,000.00

Five Thousand Dollars	XF	CU
$5000 1934A	15,000.00	35,000.00
$5000 1934B	15,000.00	35,000.00

Ten Thousand Dollars	XF	CU
$10,000 1928	—	100,000.00
$10,000 1934	—	80,000.00
$10,000 1934A	25,000.00	45,000.00
$10,000 1934B	25,000.00	45,000.00

FEDERAL RESERVE BANK NOTES

Federal Reserve Bank Notes are a type of National Currency issued not by individual National Banks but directly by the 12 Federal Reserve Banks. These are regional banks under the partial control of the Board of Governors of the Federal Reserve, appointed by the President. Unlike Federal Reserve Notes, these were legal tender but not a government obligation. The obligation to redeem Federal Reserve Bank Notes fell with the individual Federal Reserve Banks and not directly with the Treasury. They were issued for a fairly short duration.

Small-size Federal Reserve Bank Notes are actually emergency currency printed on notes originally intended to become regular 1929 series National Currency. The identity of the Federal Reserve Bank is

*1 Dollar Large Size Federal
Reserve Bank Note, Series 1918*

printed where the name of the National Bank would
have been, and small details of text are either blocked
out or added. They were issued in 1933 and have a
brown Treasury seal, unlike the large-size notes, which
feature a blue one.

Star replacement notes are scarce and command a
significant premium.

Known Counterfeits: Examine detail, silk threads in
paper and use reasonable caution.

Large-Size Notes	F	XF
$1 1918 George Washington/ eagle on flag	100.00	140.00
$2 1918 Thomas Jefferson/ battleship	365.00	550.00
$5 1915 Abraham Lincoln/ Columbus, Pilgrims landing	250.00	450.00
$5 1918 same	250.00	450.00
$10 1915 Andrew Jackson/ horse-drawn reaper and factory	1,100.00	1,750.00
$10 1918 same	1,100.00	1,750.00
$20 1915 Grover Cleveland/train and ship	3,000.00	6,000.00
$20 1918 same	1,350.00	3,000.00
$50 1918 Ulysses S. Grant/ allegory of Panama	5,300.00	9,500.00
Small-Size Notes— Brown Seal	F	XF
$5 Boston	20.00	50.00
$5 New York	20.00	50.00
$5 Philadelphia	20.00	40.00
$5 Cleveland	20.00	40.00

5 Dollar Small Size Federal
Reserve Bank Note, Brown Seal, Series 1929

Small-Size Notes— Brown Seal	F	XF
$5 Atlanta	20.00	50.00
$5 Chicago	15.00	30.00
$5 St. Louis	200.00	600.00
$5 Minneapolis	35.00	150.00

*10 Dollar Small Size Federal Reserve
Bank Note, Brown Seal, Series 1929*

Small-Size Notes— Brown Seal	F	XF
$5 Kansas City	15.00	40.00
$5 Dallas	25.00	60.00
$5 San Francisco	850.00	1,800.00
$10 Boston	20.00	45.00
$10 New York	20.00	45.00

Small-Size Notes—Brown Seal	F	XF
$10 Philadelphia	22.00	50.00
$10 Cleveland	20.00	40.00
$10 Richmond	30.00	65.00
$10 Atlanta	25.00	50.00
$10 Chicago	25.00	45.00
$10 St. Louis	25.00	45.00
$10 Minneapolis	30.00	50.00
$10 Kansas City	25.00	40.00
$10 Dallas	200.00	800.00
$10 San Francisco	30.00	65.00
$20 Boston	28.00	75.00
$20 New York	28.00	50.00
$20 Philadelphia	28.00	50.00
$20 Cleveland	28.00	50.00
$20 Richmond	28.00	50.00
$20 Atlanta	28.00	50.00
$20 Chicago	25.00	40.00
$20 St. Louis	28.00	55.00

20 Dollar Small Size Federal
Reserve Bank Note, Brown Seal, Series 1929

Small-Size Notes— Brown Seal	F	XF
$20 Minneapolis	28.00	50.00
$20 Kansas City	28.00	50.00
$20 Dallas	35.00	125.00
$20 San Francisco	60.00	200.00

Small-Size Notes— Brown Seal	F	XF
$50 New York	65.00	110.00
$50 Cleveland	65.00	110.00
$50 Chicago	65.00	100.00
$50 Minneapolis	80.00	150.00

100 Dollar Small Size Federal
Reserve Bank Note, Brown Seal, Series 1929

Small-Size Notes—Brown Seal	F	XF
$50 Kansas City	75.00	100.00
$50 Dallas	150.00	425.00
$50 San Francisco	85.00	150.00
$100 New York	125.00	175.00
$100 Cleveland	135.00	160.00
$100 Richmond	125.00	200.00
$100 Chicago	125.00	175.00
$100 Minneapolis	125.00	175.00
$100 Kansas City	125.00	175.00
$100 Dallas	140.00	250.00

CONFEDERATE STATES ISSUES

The story of Confederate paper money is in some ways reminiscent of that of Continental Currency. Under desperate wartime circumstances, and with the best intentions, the government attempted to finance the war effort by printing unbacked paper currency. The initial series, backed by cotton, held its value at first and restraint was used in the quantities issued, but as the war continued, more and more were printed, causing inflation. According to the legends on the later notes, they could not be redeemed until "two years after the ratification of a treaty of peace between the Confederate States and United States." Ultimately, the seventh and final issue was authorized in unlimited quantity. After two billion dollars were issued, the currency's value eroded almost completely. Measured in gold dollars, its decline can be seen as follows, along with rough quantities issued or authorized:

Reproduction $100 Confederate Bill

1861 March	$150,000,000	95¢
1862	$265,000,000	
1863	$515,000,000	33¢
1864	$1,000,000,000	
1865 April	*none*	1-2/3¢
1865 May	*none*	1/12¢

For many years, Confederate currency was synonymous with worthlessness, and some people even burned it. From the 1960s onward, it has taken on value as a collectible. Since the late 1990s, there has been a particularly strong market for this series. Prices have increased drastically.

The first issue of Confederate currency of March 1861 was initially issued in Montgomery, Alabama, but the wording was changed to Richmond, Virginia. This is because the Confederate capital was moved to Richmond in May after Virginia withdrew from the Union.

Throughout the war, the production of Confederate notes was plagued with difficulties. The Northern printers, who had originally been hired to print notes before hostilities erupted, were no longer available. Paper was in short supply. It was also not always practical to import notes, paper, or even plates due to the Union blockade of Southern ports. Some paper was brought in from the North by smugglers and from

Great Britain by blockade runners. As a result, some of the designs use improvised images not initially prepared for Confederate currency. More suitable images used include portraits of President Jefferson Davis and members of his cabinet, as well as of Southern agriculture.

Known Counterfeits: It has been suggested that contemporary counterfeits were made of virtually every type of Confederate currency. True or false, it stands to reason that a vast array of contemporary counterfeits of Confederate notes have survived. Most are printed from very crudely engraved plates. Like real examples, they are often printed on thin, limp paper.

Not all counterfeits made during the Civil War were actually meant to circulate. Samuel Upham of Philadelphia made 1-1/2 million Confederate and Southern state notes as a spoof, all with the notice "Facsimile Confederate Note—Sold wholesale and retail, by S.C. Upham, 403 Chestnut Street, Philadelphia" in the margin. Many had this notice cut off and intact examples are worth at least a few dollars each.

In 1954, Cheerios cereal distributed reproductions as a promotion. Other similar notes printed on brittle brownish-yellow paper were printed in the 1960s. Many but not all have the word FACSIMILE near the margin.

Some "fantasy" notes were also made to circulate during the Civil War period. These were notes

Jefferson Davis $50 Confederate Note, Seventh Issue

claiming to be Confederate, but with designs that the Confederate government never used. The most famous of these notes is the "female riding a deer" note, which actually depicted Artemis riding a stag. Most of the counterfeits, both contemporary and modern, have printed signatures. All authentic notes are hand signed except for the 50¢ denomination.

First Issue, Montgomery 1861	VG	VF
$50 Three slaves hoeing cotton	2,250.00	5,200.00
$100 Train	850.00	4,400.00
$500 Train on bridge, cattle below	1,400.00	8,800.00
$1000 John Calhoun and Andrew Jackson	1,700.00	8,000.00

First Issue, Richmond 1861		
$50 Industry and Agriculture seated on cotton	110.00	700.00
$100 Train	140.00	750.00

Second Issue, July 25, 1861		
$5 Inscription	250.00	2,100.00
$5 Liberty and eagle, sailor left	220.00	1,600.00
$10 Liberty and eagle, Commerce left	38.00	450.00
$20 Sailing ship	20.00	110.00
$20 Artemis riding stag, Indian seated left, Contemporary Fantasy	18.00	70.00

Second Issue, July 25, 1861	VG	VF
$50 Washington	22.00	125.00
$100 Ceres and Proserpina	110.00	700.00

Third Issue, September 2, 1861		
$2 Confederacy striking down Union, Judah Benjamin l.	90.00	400.00
$5 Cotton being loaded onto steamboat left, Indian princess right	1,300.00	7,750.00
$5 Commerce seated on bale of cotton	17.00	45.00
$5 Allegories of Commerce, Agriculture, Liberty, Industry and Justice, Minerva left	80.00	500.00
$5 Sailor with cotton bales, C.G. Memminger left	32.00	75.00
$5 Boy's bust left, blacksmith seated right	130.00	700.00
$5 C.G. Memminger, V at lower right	15.00	—
same but contempory counterfeit	10.00	

Third Issue, September 2, 1861	VG	VF
$5 same, but FIVE at lower right	27.00	85.00
$10 Liberty with eagle left	650.00	4,250.00
$10 Ceres and Commerce left	17.00	75.00
$10 Indian Family	80.00	425.00
$10 Cotton Picker	35.00	200.00
$10 Revolutionary War generals with sweet potatoes, Minerva standing right	17.00	75.00
$10 Wagon with cotton, John Ward left	200.00	950.00
$10 Robert Hunter left, child right	30.00	150.00
$10 Hope with anchor, Robert Hunter left, C.G. Memminger rt.	22.00	150.00
$10 same, with X X overprint	27.00	125.00
$20 Ceres between Commerce and Navigation	80.00	450.00
$20 Sailing ship	17.00	65.00
$20 Navigation seated with globe	350.00	1,800.00

$5 Commerce Seated on Bale, Third Issue

$20 Navigation Seated with Globe, Third Issue

Third Issue, September 2, 1861	VG	VF
$20 Industry seated behind large 20	12.00	50.00
$20 Alexander Stephens	40.00	200.00
$50 Moneta & chest	20.00	100.00
$50 Train	450.00	3,600.00
$50 Jefferson Davis	27.00	175.00
$100 Loading cotton onto wagon, sailor left	27.00	100.00

Fourth Issue, April 17, 1862	VG	VF
$1 Steamship	22.00	100.00
$1 same with ONE overprint	26.00	140.00
$2 Confederacy striking down Union, Judah Benjamin l.	22.00	75.00
$2 same with "2 TWO" overprint	30.00	125.00
$10 Commerce reclining	—	rare
$10 Ceres seated	—	rare
$20 Liberty with shield	650.00	3,600.00
$100 Train	27.00	75.00
$100 Hoeing cotton	27.00	75.00

Fifth Issue, December 2, 1862	VG	VF
$1 Clement Clay	26.00	85.00
$2 Judah Benjamin	24.00	75.00
$5 Confederate capitol at Richmond, Memminger right	12.00	42.00
$10 South Carolina capitol, Robert Hunter right	12.00	42.00
$20 Tennessee capitol, Alexander Stephens right	22.00	110.00
$50 Jefferson Davis	27.00	150.00
$100 Lucy Pickens	35.00	150.00
Sixth Issue, April 6, 1863	**VG**	**VF**
50¢ Jefferson Davis	12.00	38.00
$1 Clement Clay	25.00	85.00
$2 Judah Benjamin	25.00	175.00
$5 Confederate capitol at Richmond, Memminger right	20.00	38.00
$10 South Carolina capitol, Robert Hunter right	18.00	45.00
$20 Tennessee capitol, Alexander Stephens right	16.00	50.00

50¢ Jefferson Davis, Seventh Issue

$10 Field Artillery, Robert Hunter Right, Seventh Issue

Sixth Issue, April 6, 1863	VG	VF
$50 Jefferson Davis	22.00	75.00
$100 Lucy Pickens center, soldiers left, George Randolph right	27.00	85.00

Seventh Issue, February 17, 1864	VG	VF
50¢ Jefferson Davis	10.00	35.00
$1 Clement Clay	32.00	110.00
$2 Judah Benjamin	27.00	85.00
$5 Confederate capitol at Richmond, Memminger right	10.00	35.00
$10 Field Artillery, Robert Hunter right	10.00	30.00
$20 Tennessee capitol, Alexander Stephens right	10.00	30.00
$50 Jefferson Davis	22.00	65.00
$100 Lucy Pickens, soldiers left, George Randolph right	27.00	70.00
$500 Flag and seal left, Stonewall Jackson right	130.00	450.00

Index

Coins by Denomination

Paper Money by Issue

Alphabetical Listing